FINDING YOUR GUARDIAN SPIRIT

FINDING YOUR GUARDIAN SPIRIT

The Secrets of Life After Death
Revealed by Japan's Foremost Psychic

AIKO GIBO

Translated by Kirsten McIvor
Introduction by Colin Wilson

KODANSHA INTERNATIONAL
Tokyo • New York • London

Distributed in the United States of America by Kodansha America, Inc.,
114 Fifth Avenue, New York, NY 10011, and in the United Kingdom
and continental Europe by Kodansha Europe, Ltd., Gillingham House,
38-44 Gillingham Street, London SW1 1HU.

Published by Kodansha International, Ltd., 17-14 Otowa 1-chome,
Bunkyo-ku, Tokyo 112, and Kodansha America, Inc.

Library of Congress Cataloging-in-Publication Data
Gibo, Aiko, 1932-
    [Anata no shugorei. English]
    Finding your Guardian Spirit / by Aiko Gibo ; translated by
Kirsten McIvor ; introduction by Colin Wilson. -- 1st ed.
    p.   cm.
    1. Spiritualism. 2. Gibo, Aiko, 1932-   . I. Title
BF1261.2.G5313   1992
133.9--dc20
                        92-29668
                         CIP

CONTENTS

Introduction by Colin Wilson   viii
Author's Preface   xvii

Spirits Do Exist!   1
You Can Alter Your Fate   17
I Discover My Powers   25
The World of the Spirits   37
What Is a Guardian Spirit?   63
Guardian Spirits That Bring Happiness   73
Corporate Guardian Spirits   87
The Afterlife   103
Transmigration and Reincarnation   123
Taking Care of Spirits   129
Your Guardian Spirit   151

As someone who has seen spirits and heard their voices from an early age, I find it impossible to believe, as some do, that the human soul is lost with the demise of the body.

—Aiko Gibo

INTRODUCTION

By

Colin Wilson

In February 1992, I was asked by a Japanese television company if I would be willing to make a program with a Japanese psychic named Aiko Gibo. She was, they explained, one of the best known psychics in Japan, and was at present traveling around the world with a television team, making a documentary to demonstrate her powers. And could I, they asked, suggest a haunted house in England, where I might interview Mrs. Gibo? I suggested a number of haunted houses, but the one the company chose was, in fact, a haunted pub in Croydon, south London. This pleased me, because I had already conducted an investigation into the pub—the King's Cellars—and written about it in my book *Poltergeist*.

Now I should explain that my own interest in the paranormal began fairly late, when I was nearly forty years old. Before then, I had written about existential philosophy—that is, about the problem that H.G. Wells summarized in the title: "What Ought We to Do With Our Lives?" My first book, *The Outsider*, had been about misfits who feel that life is intended for something more than merely being happy. I was particularly interested in experiences of mystical illumination, when the meaning of the universe suddenly seems obvious.

When asked to write a book about the occult, I was at first skeptical, feeling that most psychic experiences can be explained as self-deception. But as I began to study dozens of cases of clairvoyance, precognition, telepathy, and poltergeist hauntings, I became aware that my skepticism had been based on sheer ignorance. The evidence for the occult was overwhelming. Moreover, since it seemed to prove that the human mind possesses powers of which we are unaware, it was also relevant to my question about the meaning of human existence.

At first I was inclined to doubt the notion that human beings survive their death; but once again, the study of hundreds of cases convinced me that the evidence for life after death is very powerful indeed.

○○○○

In 1980, when I was researching a book about poltergeists—or "banging ghosts"—I heard about the King's Cellars in Croydon, where a poltergeist smashed bottles and glasses and sometimes caused the lavatory to flush when there was no one present. On a visit to the pub, I saw this happen. But then, poltergeist hauntings seldom last for more than a few months—a year at the most. Therefore I was surprised to hear recently that the Croydon poltergeist was still active. This is why I immediately suggested the Croydon pub when I was asked to interview Mrs. Gibo.

On Sunday March 1, I waited in a hotel in central London for the arrival of the television team. They arrived about midday, and I was introduced to Mrs. Gibo. I was pleasantly surprised. For some odd reason, few mediums are physically attractive—to begin with, contact with spirits often seems to make them extremely fat. Aiko Gibo was an attractive woman who radiated good humour and vitality, and who also spoke excellent English. And as we waited for the producer, Mrs. Gibo told me how she had become a medium.

As a child, she explained, she had been silent and introverted. One of her few close friends was a pretty little girl called Ayako, with whom she often played after school. When Ayako died suddenly, at the age of six, Aiko was stunned with sorrow. She became even more withdrawn. Then one day, as she was playing alone, she heard Ayako's voice saying: "What are you doing?" And suddenly, Ayako was in the room with her.

With the naturalness of a child, Aiko accepted this strange phenomenon; it merely proved what she had always sensed: that people do not die. She became accustomed to holding conversations with Ayako, and soon discovered that her friend could foresee the future. Ayako told her that on the following day, a man would be drowned in the river. The next day, it happened, just as Ayako had foretold.

Understandably, her mother and father were deeply disturbed

○○○○

that their daughter was so unlike other children, and they discouraged her from talking about her strange experiences. So Aiko learned to keep silent about them. Her parents would have preferred her to be normal. As Aiko reached her late teens, they had their wish. Like any teenager she wanted to enjoy life and meet people. As she became more absorbed in everyday reality, her psychic powers gradually faded away.

She married a businessman, and the hard work of looking after a husband and bringing up three children turned her into a realist, who had no time for the world of the unseen. From the age of 21 to the age of 37, she had no further psychic experiences. Then, one day, it all came back. Her youngest son was four years old, and had started in kindergarten. And one day, as she was having tea with a friend named Mrs. Hayakawa, she suddenly "saw" Mrs. Hayakawa's home town, which was three hundred kilometers away. She also saw a graveyard in which one of the gravestones had fallen down, and became aware of an old man with a long white beard, dressed in a kimono, who was complaining that his grave was being allowed to fall into disrepair. She described the graveyard and the old man to Mrs. Hayakawa, who said with astonishment, "That sounds like my grandfather." But as far as she knew, the grave was in a good state of repair. Mrs. Hayakawa telephoned her brother, who lived very close to the graveyard. Soon, her brother rang back to say that their grandfather's gravestone had been torn out of the ground, apparently by a vandal.

That night, Mrs. Hayakawa dreamed of her grandfather, who was very angry. But when the grave was restored to its former state, Mrs. Gibo became aware that the grandfather was now satisfied; his spirit was again at peace.

When Mrs. Gibo told her mother that her psychic powers had returned, her mother groaned "Oh no!" and refused to speak to her for three days.

At this point in her story, Mrs. Gibo was interrupted by the

○○○○

arrival of the producer, and we went to eat a light lunch. Later that afternoon, a bus took us all to Croydon to visit the King's Cellars.

In fact, the pub had now changed its name, and was called Goody's. Since it was a Sunday, it was closed. The haunted bar is in the basement, and the landlady, a pretty girl called Tracy, took us down there.

As soon as we began to descend the stairs, Mrs. Gibo stopped and said, "I can see a man lying at the foot of the stairs." Now in fact, I had earlier broken one of the first rules of psychical research, and told Mrs. Gibo that a landlord had been found dead at the foot of the stairs. Therefore, I realized, her vision could not be regarded as valid evidence.

As we reached the bar, Mrs. Gibo stopped again and stared. "A girl has just walked across the room and disappeared through that wall." I asked her to describe exactly where the girl had come from, and she pointed to a wall behind the bar. I went behind the bar to see whether there had perhaps been a door there at some stage, but it was obvious that there had always been a wall.

I interviewed Mrs. Gibo in front of the camera, after which I interviewed Tracy, the landlady behind the bar. She told me that the poltergeist was still active—glasses often fell off the counter and broke, and on one occasion, the beer pump had begun to operate on its own, pouring beer over the floor.

At this point, the camera stopped to change film. I stood alone behind the bar, talking to Tracy. By this time, I must confess that my natural skepticism was in the ascendant, and I was beginning to feel that the whole thing was a waste of time. While I had no doubt that Mrs. Gibo was sincere, I was beginning to wonder whether she was not allowing her imagination to be influenced by what I had told her. After all, it is extremely unusual for a poltergeist haunting to last for ten years.

As I stood talking to Tracy there was a loud clink from behind me. I turned round and saw that a heavy glass had fallen

OOOO

onto the floor. For a moment, I assumed that I had caught it with my coat. Then I realized that it was too far away for that. The glasses, which stood on a ledge beneath the counter, were at least three feet away. And we were quite alone—there was no one behind the bar with us, and no one who could have reached over from the other side. Suddenly, with astonishment, I realized that the poltergeist was showing me that it existed.

I quickly called to the producer, and the camera filmed me picking up the glass. Meanwhile, a fellow researcher named Maurice Grosse, an investigator from the Society for Psychical Research, explained that he had seen the glass fall off the shelf as if it had been pushed. He had been standing at the far end of the bar drinking a glass of wine, and could see past me as the glass moved on its own.

I turned and bowed to the empty spot where the glass had fallen, saying, "Thank you." Suddenly, my skepticism had vanished.

Ten minutes later, when we had finished filming, I went across to the bar for another glass of wine. Tracy now stood talking to a woman friend, and as I listened to her conversation, I realized they were talking about the dead landlord. Now I had been unable to find any information about this landlord—even his name—and so had referred to him in *Poltergeist* simply as the landlord. Now I heard Tracy refer to him as Bernard, and I asked her how she had learned his name.

It seemed that it had happened by chance. A week earlier, the fire extinguisher had gone wrong. A label on the extinguisher gave the address of the firm that maintained it. When Tracy telephoned them, and gave her address, the girl at the other end of the line said, "That used to be the King's Cellars, didn't it? I used to work there in the sixties." Tracy then asked if the girl knew anything about the ghost. "It was a landlord called Bernard. He came in late one Sunday night, very drunk, and fell downstairs. He was found the next morning with his neck broken." Tracy

○○○○

then asked if there were supposed to be any more ghosts. "Yes, there's a girl who committed suicide. She had quarreled with her boyfriend in the pub and went back to work in the building next door. Later that day she threw herself off the roof. She landed on the roof of the pub and died."

I was excited, and rushed to tell the producer what I had just learned. Not only had we found the name of the dead landlord, but also something about the girl Aiko Gibo had seen. Moreover, we had a witness who had worked in the pub at the time, and who could tell her story on camera.

An hour later, Mrs. Gibo and I returned to our hotel, while the intrepid camera crew prepared to stay awake all night in the bar, to film any manifestations that might occur. Knowing that poltergeists are notoriously camera-shy, I felt they were probably wasting their time. In fact, the next morning, they returned to the hotel, tired and disappointed. The poltergeist had, as I expected, declined to perform.

But I, at least, had been offered proof of the poltergeist—and of the remarkable powers of Aiko Gibo.

○○○○

AUTHOR'S PREFACE

To My American Readers

This book was written both to satisfy the interest of Japanese people who wished to know more about the background of my experiences with spirits, and to bring those experiences to the attention of an international audience. In Japan my work with spirits is well known, since I have been counseling those who seek guidance for many years, and I have made many appearances in Japanese media. In this book I have attempted to explain how I came to have contact with the spirit world, how this has affected my life since I was a small child, and how it has enabled me to help others through my contacts with spirits.

Such statements as these may seem strange to some American readers. In Japan people are much more inclined to accept the presence of spirits of the dead among them than most Americans. Japanese tradition honors the spirits of ancestors, and altars to close relatives who have died are typically found in Japanese homes. The survivors place small offerings of food and drink and flowers on the altar, especially things the deceased person enjoyed in life. Important events in the lives of family members are routinely reported to the spirits of ancestors. Thus the idea that the spirits of the dead may remain close to the living, affecting their daily lives, is not as remarkable to Japanese people as it may be to those in the West, although many are not necessarily comfortable with the idea.

The fact that spirits are constantly among us may affect our lives for better or worse, depending on past relationships between the living and the dead, and on current circumstances as well. The spirit of someone who was abused or mistreated when alive may not be able to escape that situation after death, and may be said to haunt a house, building, or other location until those living there make some kind of effort to address the problem. Successful people may find unexpected troubles after changing homes or jobs, and thriving ventures may begin to fail for no apparent reason. On the bright side, the spirits of close

○○○○

relatives or friends may remain with us after death, as true guardian spirits, helping us to achieve happiness or fulfillment in life. As you will discover in reading this book, the first spirit I recognized as such was a close school friend who died suddenly, and my own guardian spirit is my dear, beloved younger brother who died when I was a child.

It is important to realize that the spirits around us are not evil demons, even when their presence may cause unhappiness. The spirits have reasons for their actions, and these can be understood and addressed by those who encounter them. My goal in writing this book is mainly to explain that spirits are a natural part of our world and our existence, and we should consider them as such. I have traveled widely outside Japan, and encountered spirits in every country I have visited, including the United States, Great Britain, and Europe. Some of these spirits were hundreds of years old, remaining trapped by some tragic fate. Others were but recently deceased, and communicated to me their wishes to help those close to them whom they had left behind. I have counseled many people, some of them world-renowned celebrities, others just ordinary men and women, but all, without exception, have enriched their lives by attaining closer understanding of the role of spirits in their lives.

I hope in reading this account of my life among the spirits of the dead you will come to understand the role of spirits in all our lives, and that this will help bring you greater happiness and fulfillment.

1

SPIRITS DO EXIST!

DEATH IS NOT THE END

As someone who has seen spirits and heard their voices from an early age, I find it impossible to believe, as some do, that the human soul is lost with the demise of the body. I have witnessed on numerous occasions the spirits of close friends and relatives separating from their bodies at the moment of death, and seen those spirits disappear into the heavens.

Often I hear messages from the spirits: things left unsaid to their loved ones, or stories they never found the words to tell while among the living. Even a simple placing together of the hands in prayer to communicate that their wishes have been heard is enough to bring a smile to their faces, and perhaps even elicit a greeting from them. It is on such occasions that the spirits are most content.

I had two brothers, with whom I got along very well. My younger brother, to whom I was very close, was involved in a fatal car accident at the age of fifteen. As children we were inseparable and could spend hours together without tiring of each other's company. I was present at the moment of his death, and the sight of his spirit departing from the sickbed and escaping through the window is one I will never forget. As this was happening he first gazed on our mother, then on each of us in turn, looking intently at our faces through half-closed eyes as if he wanted to make sure that he would not forget us. These last moments of my brother's life on earth convinced me that even when persons have departed from this world and can no longer communicate with loved ones in the usual manner, he or she still cherishes fond memories of those who are left behind.

The night after his death, when all those who had come to pay their respects had left, I stole out of the house. My mind was overflowing with memories of my brother, and I hoped that a little time spent under the stars would help to ease the pain of losing him.

○○○○

Outside our back door there was a small wooden gate, beside which stood a large peach tree. Every year the tree was weighed down with fruit, which my brother and I had enjoyed eating together. It was as I walked under this tree that it happened: for a brief second an image of the young man whose body lay back in the house flashed before my eyes. I now realize that my brother's soul was lingering there, reluctant to leave the home he had loved.

Since his death my brother has taught me a great deal about the nature of the spirit world, the hopes and dreams of those who reside there, and what they are trying to tell us. He continues to do so. My mother and elder brother have since joined him, and from time to time they send messages of their own to me. Listening to what they have to say has left me believing, without a doubt, that while flesh and bone may rot away after death, the human soul lives on.

MY BEST FRIEND AYAKO

I first became aware of my powers when I was six years old. The day I started elementary school, I found myself sitting next to a girl by the name of Ayako. Her hair, which was thick and plentiful like that of my dolls, left a particularly strong impression on me. I remember also that she had a mole on the side of her well-formed nose, which served to heighten her otherwise perfect features. Ayako's beauty was such that even a child could sense it.

Clothing was scarce at that time, and my mother was constantly changing the collar and ribbons on the sailor suit she had taken great pains to obtain for me, in an effort to brighten it a little. Ayako, however, was always beautifully turned out. She seemed to arrive at school in a different dress each day. To my young eyes her long flared skirts with frilled hems made her look like a princess.

A dress covered in blue polka dots, a pair of shiny T-bar shoes, and lace-topped socks—an unheard-of luxury—were also among Ayako's many items of clothing. They were all things that every

○○○○

little girl dreams of wearing, if only once. Her father, she told us, was the manager of a company and brought the clothes back from overseas when he went away on business.

Everything Ayako owned gave off an air of elegance. Even the eraser she used was like none I had ever seen before. In the shape of a dancer, its red high-heeled shoes formed the part used for erasing, while the rest was merely for decoration. How I wanted to use that eraser! Finally I got the opportunity: one day I forgot to bring my own, and when I told Ayako this, without a moment's hesitation she took the beautiful eraser out of her pencil case and placed it on my desk. But Ayako's kindness had long before that won my affection.

The two of us got into the habit of playing together after school. I remember rushing home and hurriedly throwing down my satchel before joining Ayako outside. Once on the street we would run around gleefully, jumping up and down on the manhole covers to see what kind of sounds we could get out of them.

On rainy days we would draw pictures and cut out paper dolls, taking turns visiting each other's house. I remember this period clearly as one of the happiest of my life.

Then suddenly, without warning, Ayako was absent from school for a day, then two days. Soon after, we were informed by our teacher, his eyes swollen from crying, that she had died of a sudden illness.

THE EMPTY DESK

Ayako's desk was bare. Each time I saw her desk I felt my breast fill with sadness as I pictured the familiar, colorful contents of her pencil case so carefully arranged upon it.

In those days, it was the custom at funerals to give each of the mourners a *manju*, which is a small cake filled with bean paste. These were a type of memorial to the recently departed person. At a time when candies and cakes of any kind were in short supply in Japan, the *manju* were particularly tasty.

○○○○

Ayako's father was hurt deeply by the loss of his only daughter, and he gave to each of us, her classmates, some *manju*, and also bags of her favorite candy. But not one of the forty of us in the first grade had a word to say when we received these generous gifts. You could have heard a pin drop in the classroom that day: none of us could bring ourselves to speak, our minds were too full of memories of poor Ayako.

That afternoon I walked home with mixed feelings, filled with both sadness at Ayako's death and joy at receiving the candy, as only a small child could be. I remember it was well into autumn, and the yellow-tinted leaves of the ginkgo trees formed a carpet on the ground. All of us went home that day absorbed in thoughts of our departed classmate. The memory of walking along dejectedly, kicking at stones with my gym shoes, is as clear to me as if it had happened yesterday.

Life was lonely without Ayako. I made no effort to make any other friends, and when my classmates invited me to play I just shook my head and returned to my brooding. It was the same at home. My life had changed completely.

I HEAR AYAKO'S VOICE

One evening, as I sat by myself playing with a doll, I heard someone calling me.

"Come on Aiko, let's play...."

There was no doubt about it. The voice belonged to Ayako.

"Wait a minute, Ayako, I'll be right there," I replied, and ran to the door of the house. My mother, startled to hear me talking to myself in a loud voice and to see me then run to the door, reproached me angrily.

"Aiko, what are you talking about? Didn't you just say 'Ayako, I'll be right there'? What did Ayako say to you? She's dead, Aiko. For goodness' sake realize that and calm down."

But standing just inside the front door, I heard it again.

"Aiko, quick! What's taking you so long? Look, I'm over here."

ОООО

How could I be mistaken? It was the voice of a friend with whom I had spent many long and happy hours playing.

Opening the door I called to my mother, "But it is Ayako, I know. She really is calling me!"

It was already getting dark outside. My mother took me firmly by the shoulders. "Come back in now," she said. "Even if you do think you heard Ayako's voice, you've made a mistake. Ayako is dead. There's no way she could be calling you."

Her face was deathly pale. Saying nothing, I retreated to my room. My mother followed and sat with me for a while. We must have stayed there in silence for twenty or thirty minutes, when my mother suddenly turned toward the window and put her hands together in solemn prayer.

"Ayako, make your way to the world of contented spirits quickly now. Don't come to fetch Aiko anymore. You can never play together again, but I pray that you will be reborn as a child destined for a long life."

From then on I spent my days in silence, talking to no one, not my classmates, my teachers, nor even the mother I loved so much. Other children would invite me to play on the slide or the jungle gym in the school playground, but to me their attempts to be friendly were simply a nuisance.

I kept up my studies, however: my father was extremely strict in this respect, and I preferred not to think what punishment might await me if I showed any signs of neglecting my school-work. So while I would only reply to the teacher's questions with a nod or shake of the head, I made sure to copy down everything that was on the blackboard into my notebooks.

"THERE'S SOMETHING A LITTLE ODD ABOUT AIKO…."

During classes, the teacher would make his way over to my desk and watch me writing, or pick up my notebooks and examine them. I remember this vividly. I also remember that he always said the same thing under his breath.

OOOO

"Ah well, she seems to be studying properly, anyway."

Not surprisingly, however, my silence troubled him, and calling my mother to the school, he asked that I be given a thorough medical examination. So I took a day off school, and went with my mother to a large hospital.

"There appears to be nothing wrong here," we were told by the doctor, an elderly man with a kind voice. "It's probably just the shock of losing her friend that has made her stop talking: just continue to treat her as you always have."

There was a storeroom in our house just inside the front door and to the left, and in it were kept several chests of drawers. There was a gap of about twenty inches between them, and when I crept into the gap my nostrils were assailed by a powerful odor, a mixture of mold and dust. I clearly remember poking the crumbling wall and watching it disintegrate into sand before my eyes. But it was in this musty place that I felt most comfortable.

As I sat there, Ayako would appear before me and say with a smile, "Aiko, there's a funeral tomorrow, did you know? I'll show you where you can go to get a *manju*." And before my eyes would appear a picture, as clear as if it were a television screen, of where I was to go.

I have been slightly deaf in my right ear since birth, and the vision in my left eye is blurred, the result of an accident. Neither of these handicaps are severe enough to be noticeable, but it is with my right ear that I hear the voices of the spirits, and with my left eye that I see their faces.

I described the visions I had as similar to watching a television screen, but in fact the colors were of a more natural hue than normally seen on film, and at times appeared faded. The directions Ayako gave me were always clear, however, and I never had any trouble finding the baker's where I was to turn right, the mailbox marking an alley I should go down, or anywhere else Ayako sent me. It was as if a moving map had been placed before my eyes. Even the hour at which the funeral was to be held was made clear to me: if, for example, the service was due to begin at two in the afternoon, the number "2" would appear in white on the "screen" before me. Funerals in Japan are generally held between the hours of ten and three, so not surprisingly, the figure which appeared always lay within these boundaries.

Knowing the starting time of the funeral, I would be unable to concentrate at school that day. I knew I had to get home, leave my satchel, and get to where the funeral was being held.

AS I WATCHED, THE DEAD MAN SPOKE TO ME

On one such day, I hurried to a funeral which was to start at two, following the directions I had been given, which consisted of turning right at a particular rice merchant's to find the large tree in front of which the service was to be held. I managed to arrive by two-thirty, by which time the place was filled with people who had come to pay their last respects to the departed.

A photograph of a plump, cheerful-looking man hung in the vestibule of the nearby house. He appeared to be in the best of health, but the picture was wreathed with black ribbon. Those sitting around it were wiping tears from their eyes. Suddenly, as I looked at the man's face, I heard him speak to me.

"Aiko," he said, "I used to have a dog called Kuro that I loved very much. Could you ask my family to put a photo of Kuro with me in the coffin?"

I agreed, but then stopped in my tracks: how was I, who could talk to no one, supposed to pass on the message? I thought for a minute, then came up with what seemed the best method. Taking a small piece of paper out of my pocket, I looked around for something to write with. Spying four or five pencils on the table where the mourners were signing their names and leaving gifts, I took one and hurriedly scrawled the message I had been asked to pass on. Pressing it into the hand of one of the family, I turned and ran home, not forgetting my *manju*, and headed straight for the secret hiding place when I got there.

○○○○

After a few minutes had passed, enough for me to catch my breath and calm down, I once again heard the voice of the plump man.

"I got the photo of Kuro, Aiko. Thank you," he said, his voice filled with joy. As he spoke his face appeared in front of me.

Even though I was only a child, I knew that the man's family had done the right thing, and it thrilled me to know that he would travel to the spirit world carrying a photo of his beloved pet. It was also thrilling to know that I had discharged such a great responsibility successfully.

THE GIRL WHO COULD ONLY SPEAK WITH THE SPIRITS

As a child I was often the subject of my parents' arguments. "I don't know what you've been teaching her, but look at her! Now she refuses to say a word to anyone."

To this my mother would reply, "Don't you see, she's just the quiet type. Just give her a few years—and in the meantime it would be nice if you would treat her a little more kindly. I'm not the only one to blame, you know."

No doubt to others I appeared to be a very lonely little girl, but in fact that was far from the case. The messages I received from the spirit world enabled me to eat lots of *manju*, and I could always talk to my best friend Ayako. I was far from lonely. On the contrary, the words directed at me by worried relations and teachers with the best of intentions were more of an irritation than anything else.

My elementary school stood on the banks of a river, and whenever anyone fell or jumped in, attempting to drown themselves, I would hear the sound of rushing water in my right ear. When this happened I would leave the classroom and go out into the corridor, following the sound, and make my way to the local police station to report that someone had jumped into the river.

My teachers had long ceased remarking on this behavior. In any case, they could hardly punish me for leaving class when they had seen the local policeman thank me for informing him of a drowning. Even now I can recall the looks of utter incredulity on their faces.

On nights after drownings, the victims would appear to me without fail in a dream. They were always anxious to tell me the circumstances surrounding their deaths and would ask me to convey certain messages to their loved ones. By now, my life revolved around the spirits and the communications I received from them.

EXPLORING THE WORLD'S HAUNTED HOUSES

So far I have spoken chiefly about my childhood, most of which I spent in the company of the spirits, but that was only the beginning of my encounters with the spirit world. Recently I was involved with the making of a television series entitled "Exploring the World's Haunted Houses," during which I had the opportunity to visit a number of haunted locations in various countries.

But my travels did not begin with the television series. I have been on many trips of my own over the years, during which I have developed a strong curiosity about how and why particular houses gain a reputation for being "haunted," as well as an interest in the real-life dramas that took place within their walls so many years ago.

Taiwan was the first place I visited, followed by Hong Kong, then Europe. By the time I had visited a large number of houses, I could detect a certain pattern in the state of the spirits within each one. Older houses are more likely to be haunted by various kinds of spirits, many of whom have degenerated into wretched apparitions. I also noticed that there tended to be many more haunted houses in countries with long histories.

Life can easily be seen as a succession of problems between the sexes, or, of problems rooted in material desire. How many people over the centuries have been treated badly by a lover or spouse? How many have been cheated out of hard-earned money and possessions? In the vast majority of cases, it is the bitterness

OOOO

and sorrow accompanying such events that cause houses to become haunted.

Europe has a long history of brutal power struggles. Over the centuries countless kings have been toppled from their thrones, and countless individuals tricked out of inheritances by unscrupulous relatives. Consequently the majority of hauntings there involve money and power conflicts. Houses never become haunted without good reason, but as a direct result of tragic events in the past.

PLACE-BOUND SPIRITS: THEIR TRAGIC APPEALS TO US

My ears are often assailed by the pleas of lonely spirits as soon as I arrive at a house with a long history. Since the spirits are desperate to speak to someone, I have little choice but to listen.

The voices of spirits which inhabit haunted houses are without exception tinged with sadness and pain, some to such an extent that I want to cover my ears and shut them out. Occasionally, just standing in front of such a house, I have felt a chill as if a bucket of cold water had been thrown over me, or I've found my legs frozen into position, unable to move.

When such things occur, I know that what I call the place-bound ghosts of the house are making their presence felt. These are the ghosts of people who have died in their homes and then were unable to leave.

Of all the activities human beings engage in, I consider war to be the most despicable. Over the centuries, millions have been sacrificed in the carnage of war, and I have often witnessed the spirits of these victims wandering the places where they were killed, unable to find rest. Without war, many suffering souls and haunted houses would not exist, and this seems to me as good a reason as any to ban all such murderous, senseless conflicts. The idea of war fills me with such anger and sadness that there are times when I want to vent my feelings in a voice loud enough for all the world to hear.

○○○○

Because I am able to communicate with the spirits, they tell me what took place in their particular area, that is, the reason for their inability to be content. For those not able to speak with the spirits directly, finding out such information is a matter of investigating the history of their house and neighborhood. If some tragic event did take place that involved a person who lived in your home or somewhere nearby, place a glass of water in a corner of a room as an offering, and put your hands together in an attitude of prayer as you think of the spirit concerned. Your actions will do much to comfort the place-bound ghost.

Spirits will at times seek help from the living, or appear to show resentment toward them, by causing confusion or unhappiness. Appeasing such spirits in the way I have mentioned will earn their gratitude, and most likely a cessation of all troublesome activity, enabling the inhabitants of the house concerned to lead normal lives again.

THE SECRET CHRISTIANS OF UNZEN

I once paid a visit to Unzen, a region famous for its hot springs. No one who travels to this area could fail to be impressed by the mysterious sight of clouds of steam rising from among the green hills.

For this visitor, however, Unzen's beauty was overshadowed by a scene of a more sinister nature. Below me in the steam I could see a group of people in white clothing; they were being pushed roughly along by men who appeared to be officials of some kind. I soon realized that what I saw was a vision of an event that was not actually taking place, but even so the scene frightened me.

As I watched, the prisoners in white, who were tied together with a rope forming a cross on each of their chests, were led to the rim of a bubbling pool and pushed in one by one. Fear and sadness gripped me, and I was rooted to the spot, unable to tear myself away from the nightmarish scene. As they were thrown into the pool I heard each of them shout "Amen!"

oooo

13

With this, my suspicions were confirmed. I was witnessing the infamous suppression of the "secret Christians" of Japan.

At the time I was gathering material for a magazine article and had a photographer with me.

"I can see some secret Christians over there, can you see them too?" I asked him. As I described what I had seen, I was choked with emotion, and tears began to roll down my cheeks.

He had seen nothing but looked disturbed and continued to take photo after photo in what seemed an indiscriminate manner.

Seeing their tangled hair and gleaming eyes, I realized that the prisoners were seventeenth-century secret Christians. Their faces showed no signs of fear, only unshakable faith. Turning toward the scene that only I could see, I placed my hands together in prayer and bowed my head, remaining in that position for quite some time.

How many years have passed since that day, I wonder. Recently that same Mt. Unzen erupted, burying a large number of people under a vast lava flow. I am certain the place-bound ghosts I saw that day are still there.

When I think of the number of place-bound ghosts crying out for help, I cannot help hoping that more people will become aware of the existence of these wretched souls and say a prayer for them. Given the care and attention of the living, perhaps even the scene I saw that day at Unzen will change a little for the better.

THE APPEALS OF UNHAPPY SPIRITS

Over the years I have encountered many unfortunate spirits, not just those at Unzen. Among them are the spirits of those who committed suicide by drowning themselves in the river near my old school. Some take great pains to point out why they chose to take their own lives. "I was lonely," they say, or, "I wanted my family to love me more," or perhaps, "I didn't have the determination to complete a task." But all of them conclude their stories by telling me they made the wrong choice when they chose to die.

○○○○

"I can't gain entry into the spirit world like this," the spirits would say to me when I was a child. "Send me some love, say a prayer for me, please—that would make me feel much better."

Not all spirits are sad, of course. Many are exactly the opposite. One I remember well is that of an elderly lady in our neighborhood who passed away after a joyful and fulfilling life. She was a kind woman, well loved by her family, and she died peacefully, surrounded by those closest to her. After her death I often saw her tending the garden she had kept so beautifully, or walking her dog.

People whose families have taken good care of them and have made them feel loved and valued always seem to be smiling and contented when they appear before my myopic left eye.

CONTENTED SPIRITS EXPRESS THEIR GRATITUDE

The type of contented spirits I have just described never come to me troubled and unhappy and never need me to do anything for them. On the contrary, I can tell that they are constantly watching over the children and family they left behind, doing their best to protect them.

Furthermore, every one of these spirits appears to be free of anxieties, such that one wonders where the pain and troubles they doubtless suffered before their deaths have vanished to.

They feel grateful to their families for every little service the family performs, even if it is only saying a simple prayer or putting aside a small portion of their favorite food on the edge of the family table.

Spirits know when something is being done for them and as a consequence will draw closer to the living. If, for example, thinking of a departed loved one who liked roses, a person places a vase of them on a table in the house, saying, "These are for you," or words to that effect, the spirit of the person in question will be pleased and will stay close to the one who has taken the trouble to comfort it.

Observing the actions of spirits toward the living, it is not difficult to tell which spirits are content and which are not.

If you have always thought that there is nothing after death, think again. And if you want to lead a happy life, you must realize how far such simple actions as saying a prayer, or making a small offering to those who have departed, can go toward brightening your everyday existence.

Your loved ones may have passed out of this world and into the next, but they still want you to be happy, and they will do all they can to ensure that you are.

2

YOU CAN ALTER
YOUR FATE

WHY DO GOOD PEOPLE HAVE BAD LUCK?

We have all heard people say things like, "Why did something so terrible have to happen to a good man like him?" or, "Why did this happen to me? I've never done anyone any harm!" If that sounds like you, I'd like you to ask yourself the following: do you know what your ancestors of two or three generations back were like?

We humans are troubled creatures, prone to being led astray by our emotions. Even if a person feels he or she has led a blameless life, that is not to say that one of that person's ancestors was not cold and uncaring, or lacking in respect for the spirits. By way of example, I shall begin with the story of two young boys who suffered from extraordinarily bad luck through no fault of their own.

A family by the name of Hayashi lived in a large house in our neighborhood. They were known as the "local millionaires." The family employed a full-time gardener for their spacious property, and he did a marvelous job of maintaining the grounds; the ever-changing display of flowers in their garden brought great pleasure to everyone in the neighborhood. As for the house itself, it was a real mansion, big enough for the family to employ three live-in servants.

The Hayashis had a son named Katsuo. He was an only child, and how the rest of us envied him. After all, we came from poor families where we had to fight with large numbers of brothers and sisters for our parents' attention. When Katsuo left the house there was always a servant to see him off with a deep bow. A limousine brought him to school, a luxury quite unheard of in those days.

One year the Hayashi household was visited by a sudden and devastating tragedy: Katsuo's parents became ill and died in quick succession from a contagious disease. The husband's younger brother and his family moved into the home a week after the

○○○○

young couple were buried, and it was not long before tragedy struck again.

The family had two sons, the eldest being the same age as Katsuo. Katsuo was far brighter than his cousin, however, and passed every one of his exams with flying colors, winning entrance to all the most prestigious schools.

When it comes to entering junior high school in Japan, all parents hope that their children will gain entrance to a top-class institution. It must therefore have been difficult for the younger brother's wife to watch the son of her deceased brother-in-law do so well while her own son struggled to pass his exams. She began to pick on her young foster son, telling him he studied too hard, or that there was no need for him to go to a prestigious school. In a particularly spiteful move, she converted a tiny storeroom in the northernmost corner of the huge house into a room for the boy.

The family appeared to have forgotten the promises they had made to Katsuo's parents to take care of the boy in exchange for considerable wealth and property, and instead seemed determined to make life miserable for him. The exact nature of their mistreatment of the boy remains a mystery, but I remember that Katsuo began to look haggard and pale, and seemed a completely different child. According to the servants, Katsuo was never strong to begin with, and even when he lay in bed with a fever, they refused to give him any medicine. Such heartless treatment aggravated a cold which he already had, and the unfortunate boy slipped quietly from this world.

IT WAS AS IF A CURSE HAD BEEN PLACED ON THEM

The two sons of the family were the complete opposite of their parents in terms of personality. They were friendly boys, and everyone in the neighborhood was quite fond of them. Eventually of course they grew up, and both moved out of the area.

Awaiting them, however, were lives so filled with bad luck it

oooo

was as if someone had put a curse on them. The older boy started a business with money his parents had given him, but just when it seemed to be up and running, the shop was taken over by someone he had thought was a friend. He soon found himself overwhelmed with debts.

The younger brother also went out on his own, only to have the house he was renting burn down in a freak accident.

Coincidence perhaps? Not when the day the elder brother was cheated out of his business and the day the younger's house burned down were both anniversaries of Katsuo's death.

The desire to leave even a little something to one's children is surely universal. But if in the process you sacrifice another's well-being, there is no way your children will be able to have happy lives.

FORGOTTEN SPIRITS APPEAL TO THEIR DESCENDANTS

That is one example of why good people may suffer from bad luck. Here is another matter concerning the spirits that deserves our consideration. There are those who, caught up in the hectic round of daily life, neglect to visit their parents' graves, and also those who, once their parents have died, are indifferent to the deaths of brothers and sisters or even to their very existence.

There are many spirits neglected by their families, who, finding the pain of their loneliness unbearable, are crying out for their families to send them a loving prayer. Without such care, helping their descendants achieve a richer and more enjoyable life is the last thing they will consider.

If people are able to live happily while ignoring the existence of their ancestral spirits, those forgotten spirits will be left to suffer the pain of loneliness during their journey through the afterworld.

Such spirits therefore try to capture the attention of their descendants while they believe there is still a chance they will be remembered. Generally they will work toward this aim until their families wonder, "How could so many bad things happen at once?" and eventually, "What is the spirit of one of my ancestors trying to tell me?" This is when people are apt to say, "Why has something so terrible happened to such a good person?"

Think back as far as your grandparents' generation. Do you have any aunts or uncles who died at a young age? If you can think of any, it is not too late. The spirits are always ready for your kind thoughts and offerings. It is quite simple: all you have to do is gather a few wildflowers and place them in a glass at one end of the table, along with a glass of water. As you do this, don't forget to say to yourself, This is for all the spirits that I had forgotten.

PEOPLE WITH GOOD LUCK, PEOPLE WITH BAD LUCK

An encounter with one of life's setbacks or triumphs leads most of us to think about our destiny. There are those whose luck seems to be strong, in other words, some people who have consistently good fortune, while others never seem to do well in any of their endeavors: their luck could be called weak. The ancestors of those blessed with good fortune are likely to have been people who made sacrifices to help others and had great respect for their own ancestors. Thus they managed to build up a store of good fortune for their descendants.

It follows that persons who think their luck is strong should do all in their power to maintain that deposit of good luck for their own descendants. This can best be achieved by sending loving thoughts to one's ancestors and by not harboring feelings of resentment or ill-will toward the living. Never forget that it is the way we live our lives that is crucial in determining whether our descendants will be blessed with good luck or not.

If we lose sight of this fact and get carried away by a run of good fortune, neglecting to care for other people in the process, we will quickly use up the store of luck left to us by our ancestors, and our own descendants will lose any chance of enjoying it.

As humans, however, on occasion we commit great wrongs

○○○○

without being aware of what we are doing. It is vital, therefore, that we take a critical look at ourselves on a regular basis, and also that we never forget to feel thankful toward our ancestors.

We all know someone who often wins lotteries, or who always bets on the right horses. Make no mistake, this type of luck has nothing to do with the beneficence of the spirits. So if some of my readers are thinking of paying homage to their ancestors, only to rush out and buy lottery tickets, I can tell them now not to waste their time. The two are simply not related. As far as I can see, the type of luck that enables people to pick a winning number is often of a transitory nature and is of no great significance.

There is a common Japanese expression that can be translated literally as, "to be directed by a devil"; it refers to a malicious thought or action so uncharacteristic of a particular person that it is assumed the person has been influenced by a devil. The expression is not to be confused with the English, "the Devil made me do it," which is in a somewhat lighter vein. I have always thought that the Japanese expression had a strong flavor of the supernatural about it.

There are those who blame problems brought about by their own carelessness on a devil who, they claim, has somehow possessed them, but this is nothing but a gross avoidance of responsibility. When, on the other hand, a mishap befalls someone who is always extremely cautious, then the expression "directed by a devil" can really be said to apply.

When a person considers a particular problem in a calm and collected manner, his or her guardian spirit will do all it can to help the person make the best decision. Persons making a decision while in a highly emotional state, or when feeling extremely pressured, are far more likely to err in their judgment. It is not that a devil has entered them and is hindering their ability to make a correct decision, but rather that they have got themselves into a state where their guardian spirit is unable to watch over them.

It follows that in order to avoid being "directed by a devil," one must breathe deeply and stay calm, no matter what the circumstances. Where malicious or resentful spirits are involved, however, we are particularly vulnerable and must make an extra effort to keep a cool head.

We are also liable to make bad decisions when our ancestors have failed to build up a store of respect for the spirits—this means we will have no strong guardian spirit to assist us.

People often speak of something happening by chance, or claim that they are destined to have bad luck, but everything that takes place during the course of our lives is related in some way or another to the vital connection between ourselves and our ancestors.

It is not too late to change your life for the better. Try taking care of the spirits of those close to you who have passed away. Make small offerings to them. The spirits really are kind beings, who will receive your messages of love gratefully and do their best to guide you and relieve your burdens a little.

3

I DISCOVER
MY POWERS

THE IMPORTANCE OF MAKING OFFERINGS AT TIMES OF UNCERTAINTY

Making my name known throughout the world has never been one of my aims in life. On the contrary, I prefer to work behind the scenes. Reading quietly at home or looking at paintings is more my style, and I admit to having mixed feelings about my recent prominence in the Japanese media.

If not my name, there is, however, something that I do want as many people as possible to know: that we all have the potential to lead better lives, and that it is a great shame to miss out on this happiness by not recognizing the presence of the spirits and conveying our love to them.

Having heard directly from the spirits what they want from us, and knowing how simple it is to make them happy, I have striven to convey this message through books, magazines, and television. While educating others about the spirit world was my only intention, in recent times matters seem to have been taken out of my hands, and the result of my activities has not always been what I expected.

I discovered my powers at the age of six: until then I suppose I was too young to express myself well enough for adults to notice them.

I SAW SOMEONE WHOM MY FATHER COULD NOT

Before I started elementary school, I remember that my father used to take me to see plays on starlit nights. Going to the theater was one of his favorite pastimes. There is a reason why one of these outings has remained so clear to me.

"Look, Papa, there's a man walking over there," I remember saying on one such outing, tugging at the sleeve of my father's coat. "There's a lady too."

"Is there something wrong with your eyes? I can't see anyone," he replied, refusing to pay any attention to my persistent tugging.

○○○○

Years later, I realized that I had seen spirits not visible to my father.

Sometimes when I was playing by myself in a nearby park, a man in a black frock coat, with the brim of his hat pulled down over his eyes, would appear before me. On those days I would go home with a fever. I still have no idea who he was, for he never spoke a word, but I certainly did not want to see him—he seemed very tall, almost seven feet to the child that I was.

Later I entered elementary school and was much the same as any other child of my age until, as I have described, the death of my friend Ayako brought about events which changed my life.

I was a child who rarely spoke to anyone, but occasionally I would surprise those around me by coming out with the most unexpected comments.

ON THE TRAIN ONE DAY

I often accompanied my mother when she took the train into town to do her errands. I liked to sit beside her, with both hands on one of her knees, snuggling up against her. When I did this, she would put her arm around my shoulder. This was the way we always sat.

One day, however, I did something different. Wriggling out from under my mother's arm, I hurried to where the lady across from us was sitting.

"You're going to have an accident soon," I told her. "Please be careful." It was quite an impertinent thing to say, but it somehow just slipped out of me.

Startled, the lady was at a loss for words and just stared at me, wide-eyed. After all, she had never seen me before in her life.

My mother hastened to apologize. "I'm terribly sorry, I don't know what made her say such a thing," she said. "Please don't give it a moment's thought."

Thus reassured, the lady smiled and patted my head.

Finally the train arrived at her stop. As she went to get off, I ran toward her again and repeated my warning. This time she

oooo

glared at me angrily and alighted without a word.

I was not very popular with my mother that day.

"You mustn't say such things to people you don't even know," she scolded. "No treat for you today."

Some time later, when the incident had been all but forgotten, we set out once again on the train. A woman on crutches got on, her leg bent and heavily bandaged.

My mother and the woman caught each other's eye and stared, both at a loss for words. Finally my mother stood up, and the woman moved reluctantly to her side, dragging her injured leg.

"Just after your daughter warned me, I was cutting back the bamboo in the garden when I fell over and landed on the stumps, injuring my leg terribly. It was my own fault, but if I'd listened to your little girl it would never have happened. You couldn't let me know your address, could you?" she asked pointedly.

This woman was later to pester me for some time, coming to ask my advice on anything and everything.

COUNTING THE PAIRS OF SHOES WHEN I GOT HOME

Stories like this one gradually spread around the neighborhood, with the result that people began coming to see me about their troubles. My mother was unsure of what to do. She tried to keep people away by telling them that she wanted to bring me up as a normal child, or that we didn't "do that kind of thing in this house." But faced with visitors in obvious distress and begging for help, she found it very difficult to decline, and finally resigned herself to the situation.

"Aiko, could you give this person some advice?" she would ask, as if it were the most natural thing in the world. When my father found out what was going on, however, he was furious.

"I don't care who they are," he fumed. "You will refuse to see any of them."

Consequently, when my father was around, my mother refused all requests for help. It must have pained her greatly to do so: she was a person of great compassion who found it difficult to say no to anyone in distress. I often saw her moved to tears by other people's suffering, even when she had only read about it in books or in the newspaper.

I found the constant stream of visitors more of a bother than anything else and did what I could to get out of talking to these uninvited guests. I seemed to have no trouble coming out with rash statements about people I had never met before, but sitting down and listening to their troubles was another matter entirely.

When I got home from school, I would count the pairs of shoes left inside the front door of the house, and if I spied any that did not belong to my family, I would stay away until late at night. I was often extremely hungry by the time I finally came home, but hunger was preferable to having to deal with all those people.

A mile or so from my house was a small hill. I would climb this hill and sit in a clump of bushes, and, if I stayed still, Ayako's voice would come to me and tell me many useful things: where a funeral would be taking place, the cause of death of the deceased, what to do in order for the spirit to be content. I came to learn more from the spirits than I had ever learned from school.

TAUGHT AND PROTECTED BY MY DEAD BROTHER

As I have mentioned, I had a brother who was two years my junior. We got along very well as children and often played together. I was not always the kindest of big sisters though, and frequently managed to trick him out of treats that our mother had given him! If I said, for example, "Let's read a book," his reply would always be yes. He never disagreed with me. As a two-year-old, he was frequently the victim of pranks perpetrated by his shrewd older sister. In fact, until I started school our relationship could only be described as that of a master and servant.

This same little boy died at the age of fifteen. Along with my older brother who died during the war at the age of twenty, my mother who died a few years ago, and my friend Ayako, my brother has sent many messages to me over the years and continues to advise me in a way I can easily understand on matters concerning the spirit world.

I am constantly grateful for the protection of these four spirits. If it were not for them, I believe a sickly person such as myself could never have survived this long.

At twenty-one I suffered from kidney trouble which almost killed me, and while pregnant with my daughter I was again gravely ill. I actually lost my powers for seventeen years after the kidney problems, and if it had not been for my guardian spirits, I have no idea how I would have coped with my troubles over those years.

I found after recovering from my illness that my irksome powers had gone, and for the next seventeen years I lived the life of an ordinary mother and housewife. I know, however, that the same guardian spirits who had helped me during the years in which I was able to communicate with the inhabitants of the afterworld continued to do so even after I lost that ability. When my psychic powers returned, I resolved to do my utmost to make others understand them.

MY DESIRE TO TELL PEOPLE ABOUT THE SPIRITS

There are those who do not take the idea of spirits at all seriously. They can't see spirits, they say, so why should they believe in them? Then there are those who see spirits as something to be frightened of. This is, after all, the image of them most widely diffused by the media.

I was unsure how far my efforts would go toward changing such widely held views. After all, there was only one of me. But despite the difficulties, I felt compelled to tell those around me the truth about the spirit world. I made several television appearances, none of which really satisfied me.

"The spirits are not really like that at all!" I often wanted to shout, but I realized there was little I could do to change views of the spirit world that had such strong historical roots.

The producers of these programs themselves had trouble deal-
ing with the topic: forced to create an image of something which
they could not see and in fact knew nothing about, they inevitably
created programs that reflected in tone and content their own pre-
conceptions of the spirit world.

"It must be wonderful to be able to communicate with the
spirits and know things other people don't," I am often told.
Don't you believe it. Just telling people about my special gift is
enough to ensure a cool reception from many.

I kept the fact that I was able to communicate with the spirits
from my children for many years. Explaining something which
cannot be explained in scientific terms is no easy task, and I believed that appearing to be a normal mother and housewife was
the wisest course.

My experiences with spirits over the years have taught me how
much the souls of the departed need our love, and I have come to
believe it my mission to make everyone aware of this truth. By
taking on this task, however, I cease to be an ordinary mother,
and I know I will be torn between a sense of mission and consideration for the feelings of my children for some time yet.

MY YEARS AS AN "ORDINARY WOMAN"

I never spoke about my psychic experiences with my husband: he
was a man who believed only in what could be scientifically
proven.

I kept my knowledge of the spirit world to myself as if it were
a guilty secret. In any case, my powers had disappeared when I
was twenty-one and stayed away throughout the years during
which I married and had children. Occasionally, articles concerning spiritualism and supernatural phenomena would appear in the
magazines I read, and I would ask my husband what he thought
of such matters, taking care to appear only mildly interested. His
reply was always the same.

○○○○

"Things like that just can't happen. People who believe them are either mentally ill or bordering on it."

For him, the spirit world was not a topic worthy of serious discussion. Faced with this sort of attitude, I decided it would be better to give up trying to talk about the spirit world, and that mentioning the things that had happened to me in the past would not be a good idea.

I bore three children, and the years passed, still with no return of my spiritual powers. The day came when my youngest turned four and entered a kindergarten. The two older children had gone to the same place, so I had no hesitation about sending the youngest there as well. When the children were off my hands for part of the day, I had thought I would like to work, perhaps at something that did not take too much of my time, but I had no definite ideas about what I wanted to do. I must admit I was very preoccupied with my children.

THE DAY MY YOUNGEST STARTED KINDERGARTEN

It happened the day I took my youngest daughter to kindergarten for the first time. At the entrance, I ran into an old friend I had not seen for years. We were about the same age and were both sending our youngest child off to kindergarten for the first time.

"Goodness, it's been years, hasn't it!" she exclaimed, adding, "You've put on a bit of weight, haven't you?"

"I suppose I might have, I've been leading such a lazy life lately!" I replied.

After a little more small talk, invited her back to my house for coffee. Eagerly she nodded her acceptance. Congratulating and at the same time commiserating with each other on the "loss" of our children, we sat sipping hot coffee, when suddenly I saw the image of a fallen gravestone appear behind my companion's left shoulder.

For a second the area behind my friend changed into a vast

graveyard, and the wall of my house into a field. The ceiling, which was white, appeared to have been transformed into a blue sky, with fluffy white clouds drifting across it. "Mrs. Hayakawa, is your family graveyard anything like this?" I enquired, describing the scene which had flashed before my eyes. Her answer came as no surprise.

"Yes it is…my family graveyard has been there for almost a hundred years. But how on earth could you know it when you've never been there?" she replied warily.

"There are some rice paddies next to the graveyard, a little above the ground, about this much," I continued, holding my hands about four inches apart. Mrs. Hayakawa sat rooted to the spot, her eyes getting rounder by the minute. "One of the gravestones has fallen over."

She had not been home for quite some time but said that if she called there now, she could speak to her brother. I offered her my phone, and she called her brother and breathlessly asked him to go and take a look at the family graveyard. Not surprisingly, she was curious to see if my vision had been correct.

Some time passed, and finally the telephone rang. It was Mrs. Hayakawa's brother, confirming that one of the stones had indeed toppled over, probably the work of street gangs, he surmised. The gravestone, however, did not appear to be his major concern.

"Who or what is this Gibo woman? How did she know such a thing?" he demanded, obviously shaken, and hung up. As his sister listened, her eyes never left me.

"Yes, exactly what kind of person are you?" she asked, and left.

THE SPIRITS RETURN TO ME

Immediately I began to worry. What should I do now that my powers were back? There's no denying it, I told myself, I've seen into the spirit world again, the visions I used to have almost every day have returned. My feelings were mixed, to say the least.

I panicked. Has the gift come back to me for good? What if

○○○○

my husband finds out? Should I tell him, and will he think I'm crazy if I do? Perhaps I should keep it a secret? But can I live with a secret like that? And what if Mrs. Hayakawa goes around telling other people? It wasn't as if I'd done anything wrong, but the children—how would it affect them? A dozen questions sprang to mind.

Finally the time came for me to fetch my youngest child from kindergarten. Unable to pay attention to the eagerly chattering child by my side, I trudged wearily home.

My spiritual powers had returned after seventeen years. I was now thirty-seven years old. From that day on, at the most unlikely times, I was plagued by uninvited visions, which persisted despite my efforts to ignore them. Before long, my children had discovered the truth about my psychic ability, which I had tried so hard to conceal from them while they were young, preferring to wait until the day when they could accept it as a serious matter.

THERE IS NO NEED TO BE AFRAID OF SPIRITS

Just mentioning the spirit world is enough to send a shiver down the spine of many people. In my view, people are making the mistake of believing a thing to be frightening simply because they are unable to see it. Having communicated with the spirits from an early age, I find it impossible to think of them as something to be feared. On the contrary, an encounter with a spirit who is being remembered and looked after by its descendants leaves me with a feeling of the deepest contentment.

As a child I read ghost stories, and listened to the stories that adults told me just as any other little girl or boy would, and I remember being extremely confused about my connection with the spirit world as a result. While the majority of spirits that appeared before me were kind and gentle, those that appeared in the stories I heard and read were without exception malicious beings, wreaking havoc on the lives of humans.

Such spirits do exist of course: those of people who have committed suicide or been murdered do sometimes turn into the horrific ghosts of our nightmares. Fortunately, however, this is a relatively rare occurrence. These spirits, and others who have been unable to make the transition into the afterlife, may remain on earth and cause problems for the living. But even these spirits can change. All it takes is love and attention from those of us still in this world.

MY POWERS AND MY CHILDHOOD MEMORIES

Here I would like to explain exactly how I discovered my psychic powers. I am almost completely deaf in my right ear: if I hold the telephone receiver to it, no matter how loud the person at the other end speaks, I won't hear a word. Likewise with music: even if it is deafening to others, my right ear remains unaware of it, as if it were stopped up with an earplug made of solid iron. My left ear is completely normal.

oooo

As for my eyes, the right one has excellent vision, and with it am able to read signs that are too far away for others to read. The left one, however, is a different story. To this day, I am not sure why I lost the sight in my left eye. I suspect, however, that the cause was an accident brought about by my now-deceased younger brother. In winter we used to keep warm around a brazier, close to which sat a pair of tongs used for grasping hot coals. One day not long before his second birthday, my brother picked the tongs up and, naturally unaware of the danger, tottered into the next room, where I was sleeping. I suppose he wanted to play. However, when he went to put the tongs on the floor beside me, the tip of them touched my left eye. I woke immediately, screaming like an animal in pain.

My mother, who had been preparing dinner, rushed in and almost fell over with shock. Sweeping me up she rushed barefooted outside, meeting my father who was just returning from work. The color draining from his face, he took me and stopped a passing taxi, telling the driver to head for the nearest hospital. The events of that day are clear to me even now.

For a year after that, my parents faithfully followed the instructions of the doctor, who told them that I would probably lose all sight in the eye but that he would do everything possible to prevent it. How many weeks had passed since the accident I am not sure, but I remember sitting at the window and looking out, my eye still covered by a bandage. I was five years old.

Not surprisingly, my mother began keeping a more watchful eye on my brother after that. The slightest whimper from me would bring her running, pale and tense, to see what was wrong.

One day I decided to take off the bandage. After all, the pain and itching were gone, so there seemed no reason to leave it on. Stealing outside, I stood under the eaves of the house and nervously removed the bandage. The dazzling flash of light at that moment is something I will never forget. The sunlight pierced my eye like an arrow, and for a second my head swam. I put the

○○○○

bandage back on, then took it off again, and after repeating this process several times my eye became accustomed to the light.

THE VIEW THROUGH MY LEFT EYE

A few days after I had removed the bandage, I began to notice that the things I was seeing with my left eye were completely different from what I was seeing with my right.

My right eye continued to see the everyday objects I had grown up with. My left eye, however, was filled with hazy images of men and women I had never seen before. During this period I was an extremely quiet child who never initiated conversation with my parents. So even though I was five and old enough to communicate what was happening, I kept these incredible visions to myself.

Looking back, I realize that if I had told my parents then, they might well have been more understanding about my ability to see the spirit world. Even my father—who believed that science could explain everything, and that anyone who thought that there was an afterlife or that spirits existed must be deluded—might have relented a little.

My mother thought along much the same lines as my father, although as a woman I think she was a little more receptive to the idea of spirits. In the end, however, she was not that different from my father in her opinions.

Although no one in my family had similar powers, there I was, a little girl who could see the spirits in her weakened left eye and hear their voices in an ear that was almost deaf. Whether these abilities only appeared after the accident, or whether I had been born with them and had simply been too young to notice, I have no idea. Either way, they have stayed with me to this day.

THERE IS ALWAYS A REASON FOR ILL FORTUNE

Whenever I look at a person who is suffering from the activities of a troublesome spirit, I can see the person's past in front of me

○○○○

as if it were on a television screen, albeit a little more faded than a television. What I see never fails to reinforce my beliefs about cause and effect, the "law of retribution" so to speak.

I am a housewife first and foremost, the kind of woman you might find anywhere. On occasion, however, when I meet a friend or a person who has helped me in some way many years previously and is now having a problem, I find myself seeking the cause of that person's misfortune. In the process, I am always surprised by the way in which past events can cause a spirit to bring ill fortune to the living.

A man, aged forty-five, who should have been in the prime of his life, came to me explaining that he and his wife were having trouble with their health. One or the other of them was always ill, he said. The couple lived in a spacious house on an equally spacious piece of land and enjoyed a lifestyle that was the envy of all those who knew them.

What should have been two contented lives, however, were dominated by the constant specter of illness. For no apparent reason the husband would find his sight going blurry and his feet unwilling to move in the direction he wished them to. He would have enormous cravings for sweet food, eating vast quantities of chocolate and whatever other kind of candy he could lay his hands on. This only served to make his health even worse. A thorough examination by a doctor revealed nothing, except that his huge appetite for sweet things was not caused by any illness.

The wife, on the other hand, was prone to fainting, and would do so once a week without fail. This happened once while she was cleaning, and, upsetting a bucket of water as she fell, the unfortunate woman caused damage to a large area of the house. She lived in fear that one day she would faint while she was cooking and would cause a fire.

For there to be no explanation for illnesses as serious as these seemed incredible. The couple had an only daughter. The girl was extremely selfish and refused to lift a finger to help around the

○○○○

house, even though her parents so obviously needed her assistance.

The husband had never believed in the existence of spirits, but those beliefs were considerably shaken by what he and his wife were experiencing, and he asked a friend of mine to introduce us. That was about ten years ago.

The couple sat in front of me. The wife in particular fixed me with a pleading gaze, which clearly expressed her desire to be free from the misfortune that had visited her and her husband.

When I am about to help someone in this way, I make a point of removing all my jewelry and any other metal objects from my person: for some reason it becomes extremely difficult to see the spirits if I leave such things on. After I did this, I turned to the couple.

Hovering between them appeared the most incredible vision. A crippled young boy of seventeen or eighteen was moaning quietly and incoherently. Keeping my eye on the vision before me, I spoke to the couple, telling them what I was seeing.

"I can see a young boy behind your shoulder there... moaning with a blank expression on his face," I began. "There is an elderly woman standing behind him: she looks worried and has her eyes on him all the time. Do either of these people sound familiar to you?" I enquired.

"That must be my wife's mother," the husband replied. "And the boy, I knew straight away who he is: my wife's younger brother."

As he said this, the elderly woman turned toward him, fixing him with a hateful glare.

ANGRILY, THE OLD WOMAN SPOKE TO ME

"This may seem rather rude, but I'm afraid this lady doesn't appear to be very fond of you," I said to the husband.

Remaining remarkably composed, he brushed off my apology. "Don't worry about offending us! If we're bringing this trouble

○○○○

on ourselves somehow, we want to know about it."

As he spoke, the elderly woman began to speak to me as well, her words slow and deliberate. "It's perfectly natural that these two should suffer," she said. "They should be in even more pain than they are now, by rights. It doesn't matter if I never make it into the afterworld, as long as they pay for what they've done." Her face was twisted with hate.

I never keep anything I've seen from people who seek my help, and this occasion was no exception. I told the couple exactly what I had heard. Stunned, the color drained from their faces.

"You'd better tell the truth," the wife said to her husband, her hand on his back. "Or we'll never be happy again." She sat with her head hanging, tears falling on her knees.

"Well, it's rather hard to talk about…" he replied, and hesitantly began to tell me the reason for the old woman's spiteful words.

From a poor family, he had come to Tokyo and worked for a grocer. His wife's family owned a large shop, which he often had cause to visit, and over time the two fell in love.

The wife's mother was a widow, and opposed the marriage on the grounds that her potential son-in-law was too poor. After much argument with her daughter, however, she was finally persuaded to give her consent. The newlyweds moved into the widow's large house.

"WE'D NEVER LIE TO YOU.…"

The wife had a younger brother who had been sickly since birth. The young man was incapable of leaving his bed or even of feeding himself.

One day the widow turned to the young couple and told them, "I'm not getting any younger, and I don't think I'll be around much longer. If you promise to look after my son for the rest of his life, you can have this house and everything I own. If you'd rather not, I'll find someone who will, and give you nothing."

○○○○

The couple replied without hesitation, "Of course we'll look after him—he means just as much to us. Don't worry, we'd never have him put in any institution. Believe us, if you're going to give us so much, we'd never lie to you."

The old lady seemed relieved, and the next day went to transfer everything she owned into her son-in-law's name. Her condition worsened steadily, and she grew weaker by the day. It was then that the young couple decided to shut her away, with the young boy, in a draughty storeroom in a corner of the house.

"Just stay in there, Mother, you look terrible," were the words of her own daughter. Regretting her naive generosity, the old lady faded away, anxious to her last moment about the future of her son. The day after her funeral, the couple placed the young man, by this time seventeen years old, in a public institution. The couple ignored the hospital's requests that they visit the unfortunate boy. They began living the high life, with no thought for his happiness, or that of the spirit of his mother, or that of the father who had worked so long to build up the fortune they were so gleefully spending.

THE SPIRITS' REVENGE

The years passed. Those who knew the couple whispered among themselves that if such things as spirits existed, then it was only a matter of time before they took their revenge. And now it had finally happened.

The wife began crying again, and hid her face behind her husband. He sat, head hanging, and occasionally let out a sigh.

"From today, why don't you start placating your mother's spirit?" I suggested. "Apologize to her, offer her some tea, if that was what she liked. And visit your brother."

The pair agreed to do as I had suggested, and left.

Several months later, I came across the couple in the street. When I enquired after their health they replied cheerfully, "Yes, we're fine, thank you. We've been doing everything you told us.

○○○○

Mother loved sweet peas, so we put some in a glass next to her tea, and we spend a lot of time talking to her."

I looked over their shoulders, and there stood the old lady once again. This time, however, instead of glaring at the couple she was smiling at them benevolently. They continued, "Our daughter has changed too: she helps us out, and soon we will have her saying a prayer for her grandmother as well. And the three of us never miss a visit to the institution where the boy is."

ANIMALS TOO CAN BECOME GUARDIAN SPIRITS

Passing before my left eye, like characters from faded films, the spirits I see are not always smiling in the way the old lady was that day. Some plead with me for help, tears running down their cheeks, while others appear to be frightened. Most want very much for their families to pray for them.

We humans are not the only living things with souls: plants and animals have them too. Most of us have felt at some time that an animal is trying to convey its gratitude for our care, even while it is still alive. When a beloved pet passes away, its spirit may remain by the side of its owner who looked after it so well. Often animal spirits are more faithful and considerate to their living masters than the spirits of fickle humans are to their loved ones left behind.

You may love an animal as if it were a child, but it is important to resist the temptation to treat it like one. Putting shoes and even clothes on a pet is going too far. My own guardian spirit, that of my brother, told me the following: "Aiko, it doesn't matter how much you love an animal, don't dress it up like a human. Animals have hair for a reason, and they've been made in such a way that they can live without clothes."

I love cats, dogs, birds, in fact any kind of animal, and will often stop to gaze at a pet whose owner has taken great care to make it look attractive. Then I think of my brother's warning and remember that such treatment is not what is best for the animal itself.

OOOO

If you look after a pet properly while it is alive and continue to send it your love even after it has died, it may reward you by becoming a wonderful guardian spirit. If you treat it cruelly, however, you may find yourself the target of that same spirit's desire for revenge.

PLANTS TOO MUST BE CARED FOR

The same rules apply to plants. It often happens that plants are left in a house for months with no one to give them water. I myself was once too sick to look after my plants, when I was visited by the spirit of my cousin, who told me to get someone else to water them, as it pained her to watch them wither and die.

Before her death my cousin had loved plants, and from the time she was a child had never been able to go out without watering those in her home. When classes finished, she would come back and sit in front of a flower that happened to be in bloom, enjoying the sight. It was no surprise, therefore, when she came to talk to me.

At home I have three flowerpots sitting by one of my windows. Receiving a great deal of sunshine, they were filled with beautiful red tulips. One day, however, I noticed that the leaves on one of them had begun to wilt slightly. Carelessly, I first watered the flower that was the prettiest, giving it a generous amount. I gave the second what little water was left in the jug, and none at all to the third plant. One day without water wouldn't hurt it, I thought, and left it at that.

The next day when I looked at the three flowers, the difference between them was startling. The flower I had lavished water on was healthy and strong, while the one I had neglected to water had begun to wilt noticeably. Without a second thought, I decided to put the wilting one away in a corner of the garden, leaving only the other two on display. That night as I slept, the voice of my cousin came to me again in a dream.

"Aiko, give that plant some water," she admonished me. "That tulip is crying, even plants have souls you know." So saying, she disappeared again, leaving me feeling horrified at my own callousness.

Since then I have come to believe that all living things have souls, and that it is important to take loving care of even the smallest plant throughout its life.

HOW PLANT SPIRITS CAN BRING YOU BAD LUCK

It amazed me to find out that, as my cousin told me, the spirit of a neglected plant can affect its owner's fortunes. Just what sort of problems can the spirits of such plants cause? Bothersome long-lasting illnesses and skin diseases appear to be common. Bad luck with money is another effect of neglect.

An acquaintance of mine filled his small garden with plants and, not content with this, crammed them into the entrance of his house as well, until there was barely room to walk. He had what could only be called an obsession with buying plants. But if they started to wilt, he would banish them to a spot under the eaves of the house and replace them with new ones. The plants thus tidied away would gradually lose all their leaves and wither completely until only dry earth remained.

This group of forgotten plants under the eaves increased steadily in size. At the same time the family, which only a generation before had been extremely prosperous, fell into a gradual decline. It was not that they were lazy or indulged in profligate spending. Their fortune simply seemed to wither away, until they were left with virtually nothing. This was clearly a case of revenge on the part of the spirits of the neglected plants, and illustrates how it is impossible for us to ignore the importance of our relationship with all living things on the earth, not just our fellow humans. The spirits have shown me that it is only when we understand this that we can lead happy lives.

Thus not only humans but also animals and plants which remember the people who have treated them kindly, and after they have passed into the spirit world they do all they can to repay past kindnesses. As humans, our strength has limitations. But if we have a guardian spirit to show us the way, we have the potential to lead truly happy lives. Next time, before you complain about a lack of luck or success in your endeavors, try sending a prayer to the spirits closest to you.

THE PRESENCE OF SPIRITS IN INANIMATE OBJECTS

This is one aspect of the spirit world I'm sure you will find particularly interesting. There are some things that human beings manufacture, such as dolls, toys, or artificial flowers, that are so beautiful we find it hard to take our eyes off them. Paintings are perhaps the best example of this: there are times when a picture monopolizes our senses to such an extent that we feel as if our soul, longing to become part of what we see before us, has left our body.

This feeling is not as farfetched as you might think. Our spirit may actually take up residence in the object of our attention—following is an example of just such a case.

A friend of mine always wore a sapphire ring her husband had given her. She never took it off. Struck down by a sudden illness, she lay in bed and, removing the ring, put it where she could look at it day after day. As her condition worsened and she became completely bedridden, gazing at the ring became her only pleasure.

After several years of illness she suddenly returned the ring to her husband. It was as if she knew her death was imminent. When she did pass away, her husband held onto the ring and kept it on him wherever he went. From that time on he seemed to be blessed with remarkable luck. Involved in a car crash in which all the other passengers were injured, he escaped without a scratch. His extraordinary good fortune was nothing short of miraculous.

Four years later, he decided to marry again. He gave the ring to

○○○○

his new wife, thinking that his first wife would protect her in the same way she had protected him. My friend had been a very generous person, so her husband assumed that she would understand his wish. Thus the beautiful sapphire came to adorn the finger of the second wife.

No sooner, however, had she started wearing the ring than she fell ill. As she lay in a feverish sleep, her husband's first wife appeared before her in a dream. The dead woman reached out her right hand, all the while staring into the face of her successor.

"What is it you want? The ring?" she asked the spirit in her dream. The other woman nodded, so she took the ring off her finger and placed it in the palm of the cold hand stretched out toward her.

Upon completing this action, she woke, to find the room empty. There was no sign of the woman who had been standing next to her only seconds before.

She dismissed it all as a dream until she noticed that the ring was missing from her finger. Frantically she searched nearby, and found it lying under the bed. She realized then that she had experienced more than a dream, and that there was no way she could continue wearing the ring.

The following day she told her husband what had happened, and they decided that it would be better if he held onto the ring. He began carrying it with him again, and occasionally the couple would place it on the table and say a fervent prayer for the dead woman.

Needless to say, the second wife recovered from her illness. The husband is a driver by occupation, and swears that the ring protects him from harm. Thus, a spirit may take up residence in an inanimate object in order to take care of someone it cares about deeply.

THE DOLL THAT LIVED FOR CENTURIES

An acquaintance of mine who loves antiques bought a doll

that was said to be several hundred years old, while on holiday in a small town in France. It was clothed in a yellow dress and a white apron, but it was the face that made those who saw it stop and shiver. It was far too realistic, and possessed none of the child-like charm that dolls' faces normally have.

The man's family all agreed that evil was the only way to describe it, and demanded to know why he had bought such a horrible thing. But my friend had taken a great deal of trouble to bring the doll back from a far-off country, and he was not willing to part with it easily.

When he had first seen the doll sitting in the antique shop, it seemed so real he thought it was alive. While he browsed through the large array of china on display, he felt as if its eyes were following him around, watching him as he examined the bowls and plates. Normally he had no interest in dolls and had in fact entered the shop to look at the china, which was his first love when it came to antiques.

On this day, however, he found himself unable to feel enthusiastic about the porcelain, and his thoughts kept returning to the doll. It was not a pleasant feeling, and he decided to leave the shop. But the doll, it seemed, had other ideas, and he found himself drawn back inside as if he had been called. Again and again he tried to leave, and decided in the end that if he bought the doll, his uneasiness might disappear. It was not particularly expensive.

Taking his purchase back to the hotel, he packed it away in a suitcase. Again the doll seemed to call to him, this time telling him to take it out, and again he felt uneasy, but he dismissed his doubts as the result of a tired and overworked brain.

After arriving home, as I have said, he suffered endless harassment from his family about the strange doll. Whenever their jibes became too much he would explode with anger and stubbornly refuse to put the doll away. But to himself he had to admit that the doll really was frightening and seemed to become more so by the day. The other members of his family claimed that if they got

○○○○

up in the middle of the night and happened to look at the doll, it would stare back at them. He dismissed such claims as the product of their overactive imaginations, but all the same he decided to find out for himself.

Getting up at around two o'clock, he went into the living room where the doll was and sat down on the sofa to watch it. As soon as he had done so he heard a deep sigh, followed by a voice, speaking to him.

"Give me back to my owner," the doll pleaded.

Shocked, he got in touch with me the next day through a friend and brought the doll for me to see.

Once out of its wrapping, the doll began whispering in my right ear. "I don't want to belong to anyone, I already belong to Françoise."

Obviously the doll had been the beloved toy of a little girl of that name, and her spirit lived on in it, even after hundreds of years. Françoise must have died many years before, so of course it was impossible to return the doll to her.

I suggested that my acquaintance put the doll in a proper box, cover it with flowers, and bury it, all the while praying that it return to where its owner lay and protect her spirit. My friend has not heard the doll's voice since then, and the family's life has returned to normal. Even now when they get together the subject of the doll invariably arises, and all concerned wonder whether it managed to return to its young mistress.

THE STORY OF A WRAITH

Have you ever heard the term "wraith"? Generally it is used to refer to the spirit of a living person that, out of extreme hatred or resentment, haunts another.

"We were tricked into selling our land for almost nothing by a real estate agent—land that had been in the family for generations. He took advantage of us. I suppose it was partly our own fault for not having had a clue about what it was worth, but we'd like to buy it back, adding on a little commission for the agent, of course. Would you be able to get him to talk to us?"

The elderly woman who came to me with this story was obviously in despair, her face stiff with the effort of maintaining her composure. She lived with her sister. Both in their sixties, neither had ever married, and they had enjoyed a quiet life together for many years.

Their home was on the hills overlooking Yokohama, an area where the wealthy build mansions with breathtaking views of lush green forests, the blue sea, and ships sailing into port. The area is so well known as an enclave of the rich and famous it seemed remarkable that anyone should not know how much the land was worth.

"We've spent our entire lives in that house," my visitor began to explain. "So we never knew how much it was worth. Besides, we've had very little contact with people other than our family and had no knowledge of anything like land prices.

"Unfortunately, my sister has fallen ill recently, and we decided to sell half the land to pay the medical bills. As it is, the garden is too big for us and its upkeep eats into our savings.

"It was land our father had considered very precious, so we wanted to keep half of it. We heard that our neighbor was a real estate agent, so we asked him how much the land was worth. He told us that we should sell it right away, that the price would fall any day, and that he would take it off our hands there and then if we liked. He placed a pile of documents in front of us and pressed us to sign in several places.

"Well, we knew nothing about the neighborhood really, nor about anyone who lived there, but you don't think your next-door neighbor is going to cheat you.... Now we regret trusting him so readily of course, but the land is already sold, for two million yen a *tsubo*. [A *tsubo* measures approximately thirty square feet.]

"The next day we bumped into an acquaintance and told her

○○○○

about the sale. When we let on how much we had sold the land for she was shocked. The price, she said, was decades out of date.

"We were stunned, especially when she told us that the going price for land in the area was eight million yen a *tsubo*. She herself had in fact been intending to buy land in the area, and was given this figure by the very man we sold ours to. She told us it might not be too late to cancel the sale, so I rushed next door. The reception was cool: our neighbor refused to talk about selling back the land. Certainly there was a going price, he said, but there was no law laying down that everything had to be sold at it.

"In tears, I went to his wife, but she was no more helpful. It was our own fault for being fooled, she said, and in any case it had nothing to do with her. Her major concern was that we start clearing trees off the land so they could build their house.

"I pleaded with them for a little sympathy. After all, the land had been sold to pay my sister's medical bills. They stood their ground, however, and I had no choice but to head home. So as you see, I've tried appealing to their good nature, and what else can I do?" she concluded.

SOOTHING THE CRYING WOMAN

This obviously gentle and well-bred lady was at the end of her tether. It so happened that I knew the real estate agent: he had come to me some years previously to ask advice about his children. I had been able to help him out greatly on that occasion. I promised to talk to the agent and his wife.

"They have had a lot of worries of their own in the past, about their children, so I'm sure they will understand what you're going through," I said, trying to reassure the poor woman. "I'll get onto it straight away, these things are best dealt with as quickly as possible."

I telephoned the agent's wife and went to visit her that evening. Couldn't they pay the ladies a little more for their land, I asked. She refused to budge from her view that it was the sisters' fault

○○○○

they were out of pocket, not hers or her husband's.

I had hoped to avoid doing it but decided it was time to bring up the past.

"Didn't you have trouble with your children a few years ago?" I asked coolly. "Surely then you can understand what your neighbors are going through?"

I must have spent several hours there, but she was adamant that they, the buyers, were in the right, and that I was in the wrong to even question the sale. I left feeling disillusioned, wondering if perhaps I should have minded my own business instead of becoming involved.

I informed the sellers of my lack of success, and I will never forget the look on the face of the sister who had spoken to me as she declared, "I hate them, I'll hate them forever for what they've done to us."

Before long, a magnificent new house stood on the land in question. The sisters could not bear to stay where they were and be forced to see their neighbors, and they eventually sold the remaining half of the property through a different real estate agent. At eight million yen per *tsubo*, of course. Still it was little consolation, for they felt they had been virtually driven out of the house where they had spent most of their lives by the deceitful real estate agent.

The agent and his family felt on top of the world. They were the proud owners of a brand-new home, their triumph made sweeter by the fact that the land had been purchased so cheaply. Nothing could go wrong for them.

In contrast, the elderly sisters, according to a friend of mine who lived near them, spent every day in their new home seething with resentment at the way they had been cheated.

"Even though they've got a new house, they seem to spend all their time burning with resentment about that real estate agent. It's a shame to see them like that, they were such lovely people, so kind."

○○○○

My friend shook her head at the tragedy of it all. Everyone who knew the sisters rallied round and supported them, and marveled that anyone could do anything so horrible to two elderly women living by themselves and sheltered from the harsh realities of life.

SOMEONE WATCHING FROM THE SHADOWS

One night as I happened to be passing the real estate agent's new home, I spotted one of the sisters. It was after eleven, but—there she was, hiding in the grass, staring at the house.

I decided to call out to her and moved closer, but there was no sign of anyone. At first I thought she had returned because she missed the place where she had lived for so long. Her expression, however, was not one of longing or sadness, but one of pure loathing.

Several years passed, and I had all but forgotten the incident when an acquaintance came to visit, and asked if I remembered the house on the hill. I said I did, and she continued, "The wife left her husband, you know, and took the three children with her. She's having terrible problems—the oldest is almost twenty but refuses to go to classes, doesn't do any work, and spends all his time running around with his friends. I tell you, it doesn't make me feel very good, having kids hanging around outside late at night like that."

It was just the kind of thing a wraith would do, I realized at once. If the agent and his wife had mended their ways and righted the wrong done to the two sisters, and had generally lived more honest lives, they would not be having these problems. Slowly but steadily, I feared, the wraiths of the sisters were going to make life increasingly unpleasant for the pair.

WRAITHS ARE CREATED BY FEELINGS OF RESENTMENT AND JEALOUSY

As this example shows, a wraith is the manifestation of the soul of a living person who causes harm to another person. A wraith can at times be extremely frightening in terms of the power it musters to avenge a wrongdoing. Fortunately, such spirits are a very rare phenomenon.

If a person is being "followed" by a wraith constantly, he or she will feel anxious about anything and everything, until even the most everyday tasks become a trial.

Wraiths come into existence when people who have been wronged, burn with so much jealousy or resentment that vengeful thoughts occupy their every waking moment. Or, when they are filled with a different but equally obsessive type of emotion: love. It could be that for a child, or a lover. Burning love or burning hate: both are capable of producing wraiths.

Wraiths and the spirits of the deceased are by nature completely different entities.

The spirits of the dead give off no heat, they have no heartbeat. When I encounter a wraith, however, I can feel the warmth of its body and see it breathing.

The victim may not realize that someone holds such an obsessive grudge against them, but the wraith's presence will often be manifested by health problems or difficulties at work. Medical examinations will reveal no apparent cause for the victim's condition, but in the case of many mysterious illnesses, a wraith is indeed the culprit.

When I see these victims, more often than not there will be a figure standing behind them, its eyes fixed on them with a hateful glare. When I ask the wraiths why they are there, invariably they have a story of pain and resentment to tell.

Wraiths do not come into existence through everyday emotions. The kind of resentment required is so strong that it may well kill the person feeling it, and producing the necessary energy is far from easy. Consciously willing a wraith into existence in order to harm someone else in the way I have described is no simple matter.

○○○○

Wraiths have been with us since the earliest days of human existence, and I believe they are more common now than ever before. As human beings have grown in knowledge and sophistication, their relations with others have become complex, and we now have more reasons to feel resentment or jealousy toward others than ever before.

VENGEFUL FEELINGS CAN BACKFIRE ON US

Wraiths are greatly influenced by the nature of the persons from whom they originate. People who are melancholy, pessimistic, and who refuse to come out of their shell to meet others, preferring to nurse their resentments, whether justified or not, and who feel themselves victimized, are the most likely to have souls that can be transformed into wraiths.

Such people are generally very unhappy. Unable to express their feelings out loud to the person they resent, those feelings backfire on them. There are times when we would all like to have a wraith bothering someone we loathe, but what is important to remember is that in order to do so we will have to suffer as much as our intended victim.

There is a proverb in Japanese, "*hito o norowaba ana futatsu*," which is similar to the expression in English about "chickens coming home to roost," and refers to the danger of a curse backfiring on its originator. There is a great deal of truth in this saying, at least with regard to the spirit world. I have witnessed countless examples of wraiths that have returned to their originator and made life even more of a nightmare than before they came into existence.

Wraiths do not always attach themselves to the object of resentment easily. It may take many sleepless nights of continuous willpower to insure that they do.

In the end, we are better off taking care with our words and actions not to hurt others. Something said in passing may cut another person deeply, and our words may come back to haunt us in the

OOOO

form of a wraith. Acting kindly toward others at all times is, I believe, the best way to conduct our relations with those around us.

MY MOTHER DURING MY FIRST YEAR AT SCHOOL

I have one more wraith story for you to consider. In my first year at school, I ceased talking with everyone except the spirits. Seeing that her daughter was shut away in a world of her own, my mother was naturally concerned. I often ventured out by myself in spring, to scoop tiny fish out of a nearby stream or pick the wild flowers blooming in the fields.

Whenever I was about to go out, my mother would come hurrying, wiping her hands on her apron and saying, "Aiko, where are you going? If you're going to the stream, make sure to stay away from the deep spots. And don't go too far, or you'll get lost: stick to the roads you know." So she would go on. I, however, would say nothing, and giving no indication of whether I had even heard her, would run out of the house.

One pleasant afternoon at the beginning of summer, I was chasing a butterfly through the hills. Nowadays, the spot is covered with houses, but when I was young the area was only sparsely populated, and it was not the kind of place in which a small child should have been by herself.

The butterfly I was pursuing had small white wings, like the petals of a flower, and it flew deeper and deeper into grass that grew as high as I was in those days. Just when I thought I had lost the insect, it would appear again, tantalizing me. I lost all notion of the time, until I noticed that the temperature had dropped considerably and that my arms were covered in goosebumps. Suddenly I realized I should be heading home.

Where home was, however, I had no idea. I walked and walked, along paths covered in weeds, and became increasingly frightened. Finally I sat down, exhausted, and tried to remember the way I had come. The flowers nearby suddenly seemed terribly lonely and sad.

○○○○

"I want to go home…" I said, but of course no one answered. The wind, which only a short while back had felt gentle on my cheeks, was now a chilly breeze, increasing in intensity all the time.

It was all too much for me. I began to cry.

I will never forget what happened next. Looking up I saw my mother coming toward me, hurrying through the long grass. There was no mistaking her. She wore a white blouse with a brown skirt, and her eyes, large enough under normal circumstances, had grown even wider with worry.

WHAT I THOUGHT WAS MY MOTHER

I leaped up and ran joyfully toward the approaching figure. Suddenly, it disappeared. But where it had been, the grass was parted and easy to walk through. I saw a small, broken bamboo insect cage that I remembered passing on my way up the hill.

I felt as though I had woken up from a long sleep. Following the path that had been laid out for me, I walked down the hill. The path gradually became wider and wider, until I arrived home, out of breath from running.

"Aiko, have you been up into the hills?" My mother rushed out to meet me. Instead of her usual clothes, she was wearing a new white blouse and a brown skirt.

She had been about to go out looking for me and, giving up her dinner preparations, had changed her clothes to do so. It was the first time she had worn the blouse.

Smiling with relief she told me, "I was worried you'd gotten lost in the hills, Aiko! I could imagine you sitting down somewhere trying to think where to go. I know it sounds silly, but while I was imagining you, I could see an insect cage on the ground beside you…anyway, at least now you're safe."

My mother had no psychic powers. She was always more of a believer in what she could see with her own eyes than in anything related to the spirit world. I know, however, that it was her

○○○○

wraith, born out of a mother's love and concern for her child, that guided me home that day. There can be no other explanation.

OOOO

5

WHAT IS A
GUARDIAN SPIRIT?

GUARDIAN SPIRITS WATCH OVER US ALL THE TIME

Do you ever wonder why certain people are so successful? When I meet such people, I inevitably sense that they have a guardian spirit. A guardian spirit is a spirit who watches over a particular person. Therefore, a person who has a guardian spirit is likely to be much happier than a person who is without one.

The relationship between ourselves and the spirits is one of give and take. If we show love and understanding for the spirits, they will often help us when we need their support. If you experience good fortune in your life, remember to thank your guardian spirit. This is one way of ensuring its continued assistance: no spirit could be angry with you if you express your gratitude.

What must be remembered is that not everybody has a guardian spirit: in fact, only about forty percent of us do. If you are the type of person who always manages to escape injury when others have been hurt or who unfailingly gets out of tight situations, then there is a strong likelihood that you are among that forty percent.

Who are these guardian spirits then? If you have one, it is probably an ancestor from three generations back or less. Do not make the mistake of thinking that this spirit is always with you. Much depends on how you treat it and on your way of life, and the spirit can just as easily turn its back on you.

CARL LEWIS—THE FASTEST MAN ALIVE

Some time ago I had the opportunity to meet Carl Lewis, the world-famous sprinter. I know very little about sports, and when someone mentioned Mr. Lewis's name to me, I replied that it sounded familiar, but that I wasn't sure what he actually did. Was he a musician? A dancer? A scientist perhaps? In the end I had to ask the person from the television station who had come to me with the idea of interviewing the sports star.

○○○○

"You must be the only person in the world who doesn't know who Carl Lewis is!" he marvelled.

"Good grief, is he that well known?" I replied.

"Ask your son," was the answer. "He'll know who Carl Lewis is."

I did just that, and got the merciless teasing I deserved. Carl Lewis was an Olympic gold medalist, a star of the sports world. Everybody knew who he was! Apart from me, that is.

"Will such a famous person want to meet me?" I asked someone at the television station.

"Well, we faxed him, and he seems pretty interested in seeing you" was the surprising answer. "In fact, he wants to meet you soon, if possible."

It appeared that Mr. Lewis felt no antipathy toward the spirit world, and, breathing a little easier, I threw myself into preparing for the trip. A few days later we flew to Houston, where Carl Lewis was waiting to meet us.

A TENSE AND ANXIOUS CARL

After we had arrived and rested for about three hours, Carl came to our hotel room, knocking softly on the door. I invited him in, and he entered, tense and unsmiling. After we had made ourselves comfortable, I handed Carl a large sheet of paper, asking him to write his name and date of birth on it.

This is my usual procedure before conducting a spiritual reading, as it tends to relax the subject. Certainly I do not always need a full name or birthdate, but unless the person is relaxed I find it difficult to conduct a reading, an unfortunate weakness of mine.

"Full name, did you say?" Murmuring to himself, Carl wrote his name and the date July 1 in bold letters. He still appeared tense, but as far as I could see, performing this simple task seemed to have relaxed him a little.

"I think you feel that your success in these races has been helped by something other than your own ability," I began. Carl nodded silently.

○○○○

"When you came into the room," I continued, "your father was behind you, following you. He is your guardian spirit.

"Some people have no guardian spirit, others have one, yet others have two or three. When I look at you I see two men: one is your father, the other is your grandfather. You probably don't remember your grandfather very well, but he was a very hard-working man."

Carl stared at me, his adorable eyes wide with curiosity.

A MESSAGE FOR CARL

"Yes, my father often told me about my grandfather. He was indeed a very hard-working man, and strong-willed too."

"He is protecting you," I continued. "Now if you like, I have a message from your father here.

"You always take off from your right foot, don't you? A difficult thing to do, as you know, but you also know it helps you win races."

He nodded in agreement.

"Your father is telling you to take particular care of your right ankle."

Carl's expression became even more serious.

"When you practice, you must choose your shoes carefully. Ones with a blue line on them seem to be the best."

"Yes, those are what I practiced in before I got the gold medal," he said.

Suddenly, a black fountain pen appeared n the air between us.

"Carl, did you by any chance receive a pen from your father as a gift?" I asked.

"Yes, I did."

"You haven't used it lately, have you?"

"No, I haven't. It's just locked away somewhere. But I haven't lost it."

Another object appeared before me. "A watch…a good watch, have you ever been given one?"

○○○○

My visitor thought for a while. "Ah, yes, I have. But I haven't used that for a long time either."

"Your father wants you to use the pen and watch. The watch is lost so he is asking you to get your mother to buy you a similar one. If you wear it sometimes, and if the night before a race you write "Papa" with the pen and ask him for help, you will be able to perform well."

Smiling and nodding now, Carl said, "Yes, Papa, I'll do that, I'll do that all right." He began to call to his father, as if he could see him in the same way I could. Mr Lewis, standing behind his son, smiled over the top of his glasses. There was no doubt in my mind that even from the spirit world, he was looking out for Carl.

A BRICK BUILDING

"I'll have to think about my shoes, too," Carl was muttering to himself.

As he said this, a faded brick building appeared between us. The scene was not one commonly found in Japan: a vast lawn and garden, bordered by a wide pleasant road. I think Carl's father wanted me to know the kind of place his son lived in. "The rooms in your house are not that large," I said, describing what I saw. "They are the perfect size for talking together as a family. The room where you all gather is on your right as you go through the front door."

Again Carl laughed and nodded as I spoke. "Someone in your family will want to sell this house in the future and move, but your father wants you to hold onto it. This is where he spent his happiest days, where he likes to return sometimes. I suppose the house holds a lot of memories for him of his children," I continued, an image forming in my mind of Mr. and Mrs. Lewis and their children talking happily with each other.

Spirits as attached as this to their former homes are actually quite rare. I have communicated with many spirits over the years, but this was the first time I had met one who felt as strongly as

Mr. Lewis's spirit did about the house he had once lived in.

After the reading was over, Carl asked me over to his house. The family was together for Christmas, and they were looking forward to meeting me, he explained.

Along with my staff, I accepted the invitation and drove home with Carl. Although it was only six in the evening, it was already pitch black outside. Eventually we arrived at the house I had seen earlier. Christmas lights flashed on and off, guiding us in from the darkness, and the impression was one of a friendly household aglow with seasonal festivities.

Carl ushered me into the house. His mother, dressed in a lovely red blouse, came to the door and welcomed us. Carl's younger sister Carol showed us around. There were many photographs on the walls, an expression of the warmth of the Lewis family's ties of affection. For a while, I must admit, I was taken aback by the dazzling decorations—this was a rare opportunity for me to visit an American home in the midst of the Christmas festivities.

Carol brought out a photo of Carl when he was five and showed it to me: a lovely little boy whose black-framed glasses made him look older than his years.

A MESSAGE FOR HIS BELOVED WIFE

A little later I conducted a spiritual reading with the whole of the Lewis family present. Usually when I begin a reading, the spirits try to speak to me by causing images of people and animals, even objects, to appear in the air before me.

On this occasion, a shiny object appeared before Carl's mother, accompanied by the deep voice of her deceased husband in my ear. "I bought them for her," he was saying, "but she never wears them, not even at Christmas."

"Mrs. Lewis," I enquired, "did your husband ever buy any jewelry for you? Perhaps as a Christmas present?"

"Yes, he did," she replied. "A pair of diamond earrings. But I was afraid of losing them, so I shut them away in a drawer. I sometimes open the box and have a look at them though."

"Your husband wants you to wear them, you know. He says they will help Carl greatly. Please," I continued, looking at each member of the family, "if either your father or I say that a particular object you own is lucky, I'd like you all to wear or carry that object with you from time to time. And Carol, you could go far in the sports world as well. All you need is to practice more, your father says."

Carl took up where I left off, exhorting his sister to practice, though smiling broadly as he said it. Carol made no reply, answering only with a wry grin. I continued, "Carol, I can see horses associated with you."

"Really?" she replied, startled. "I love horse riding. I've been trying to get Mom to buy me a horse, but she refuses."

Carl added, with a mischievous laugh, "Yes, that's right, Carol loves horses. But I can't stand them! They scare me, they're far too big, and I'm sure I'd get thrown if I tried to ride one!"

"Your husband is asking you to buy Carol a horse, Mrs. Lewis," I continued. "That's why he is urging her to practice."

"Come on, Mom, buy me a horse," pleaded the girl.

"Well, we'll see," Mrs. Lewis replied, with a look that said she was unable to refuse her children anything for too long.

"Leave it to me, Carol. I'll get her to buy you a horse," added big brother, looking at his sister with affection.

"So, will this year be a good one for the Lewis family?" Carl's mother turned to me again.

"Well," I considered, "if you do the things that I have told you to do tonight, then it most certainly will be."

Everyone greeted this statement with smiles. I could tell that this was a close-knit family, and that Carl took great care of his mother. A guardian spirit finds this kind of family easy to look after.

WAVES APPEARING IN FRONT OF MR. LANDIS
On the edge of a quiet hillside suburb in Yokohama live a family

○○○○

by the name of Landis. Mr. Landis is employed by a Japanese company, and when he first came to the country, ahead of his family, he got to know one of my friends well. This friend invited me to dinner one night, and Mr. Landis was also there. It turned into an evening I'll never forget, even though the events I am about to describe happened many years ago.

The moment I saw Mr. Landis, I was struck by a vision of a wave, like a tsunami, swelling in front of him. The roar of it filled my ear. Thinking it rude to disclose something like this to a person I had only just met, I continued the conversation I was having with my friend Michiko about the theater. The sound continued to filter through, however, and I began to worry.

Enough was enough, I finally decided, and cutting off my conversation with Michiko, I turned to our companion.

"I know this is a rather strange thing to ask you," I began, "but is your home in America near the sea by any chance?"

"It most certainly is," he replied. "The location is marvelous, right by the edge of a cliff. We can see mountains in one direction and watch the waves crashing against the cliff in the other—it really is beautiful. My family is coming out here from California soon." He continued, a little concerned, "Has something happened to them?"

"It's difficult for me to say something like this to someone I don't even know, but frankly, I'm extremely worried about your family's safety. Please call them in the next couple of days, and tell them to be careful of water. And a dog..." I then asked, "Do you own a brown fluffy dog about this big?" I held my hand a yard or so from the floor.

"Yes, we do!" he replied excitedly, raising his voice. "Is it all right?"

"I would like that dog to be careful of water as well."

My friend's husband interjected hastily, explaining to the guest that I possessed powers that enabled me to see into the future sometimes.

○○○○

A CHILD ABOUT TO DROWN

Mr. Landis's expression suddenly changed. Surprised, he was obviously finding his host's explanation hard to believe.

A month later, I met Michiko again.

"Remember that evening at our place, when you warned Mr. Landis about water?" she enquired. I had already forgotten, but her words jogged my memory.

"There was a tsunami near his house!" she continued excitedly. "His wife and children just managed to escape with their lives. And the dog saved one of the children from drowning—grabbed it by the shoulder and pulled it to safety. It died three days later, almost as if it had given its life for the child's."

Mrs. Landis and the children had apparently arrived in Japan still in a very distraught state.

Later I had a chance to meet them, at Michiko's house. When I mentioned the dog, the little boy, only six, began to cry. His shoulders shook with grief.

"He was my dog," he sobbed.

People tend to think of guardian spirits as being those of humans, but this is by no means always the case. I believe it was the dog, Daniel, who sent that message about water to me while he was still alive.

6

GUARDIAN SPIRITS THAT BRING HAPPINESS

KATHY AND HER TWO MOTHERS

A woman by the name of Kathy, whom I met in San Francisco, revealed that she was troubled by the following problem. "I was brought up in an orphanage, so I've never seen my real parents, not even in a photo. But from what my adoptive parents have told me, my father was a lawyer and my mother a teacher. Both were from distinguished families, and the shame of having a child out of wedlock was too much for them, so they put me in an orphanage.

"My adoptive parents had no children of their own, and they were very kind to me. I married a good man—my husband is generous and understanding, and I'm very happy. I suppose you think I have no right to be worried about anything, but now that I've turned forty I've started feeling a strong desire to know about my natural parents. If you know anything, please tell me, even the slightest details."

I found myself in a dilemma. I had realized by this time that what Kathy's adoptive parents had told her was not true.

While Kathy was talking to me, a figure had appeared behind her. It was her adoptive mother, now deceased. I cautioned the anxious woman sitting in front of me.

"Kathy, if you think you can take it, I will find out the truth. But it might be better if you didn't know."

"Mrs. Gibo, that's all right. Nothing could surprise me. I remember my time in the orphanage well, and I know what good people my adoptive parents were. I've had a happy life so far, so no matter how sad it is, it won't upset me."

So be it, I thought, and began to speak.

"All right then, Kathy, I'll tell you what I see. Your adoptive mother is telling me that you should know the truth. First, your father. He was a machinery salesman from South America.

"Yes, yes, my adoptive mother told me my real father came from there!" Kathy interjected excitedly.

"Well, yes," I continued. "But he wasn't a lawyer. You must

○○○○

75

feel a little let down. And your mother, she was a waitress in a bar and came from North Carolina. They fell in love here in San Francisco, and you were the result. Unable to bring you up, they left you in an orphanage and disappeared. But the people who adopted you loved you very much, didn't they? I think you have led a very lucky life."

Kathy nodded, adding that she had often heard the name North Carolina mentioned by her adoptive mother.

"It was just their jobs that were different," she said, hanging her head.

"Kathy," I added, "you're old enough to hear the truth about your parents. That's why I told you exactly what I heard from your guardian spirit. That's the mother who brought you up, and the one you should feel most thankful toward."

CARNATIONS

Kathy lifted her face to me, her eyes glistening with tears. Quietly she began to speak. "All these years I've been longing to meet my real parents, never thinking to thank the people who brought me up. I've taken them for granted."

"Kathy, your adoptive mother loved pink carnations, didn't she?" I asked. "So even if it's only one flower, put it in a glass for her, and pray that she will be happy in the spirit world. And don't forget to tell her how grateful you feel to her for bringing you up. She will be very thankful."

She promised faithfully to do what I suggested, then asked me another question.

"Mrs. Gibo, my husband and I want to move. Will we find a good house?"

"Try asking your mother when you give her the carnations," I replied. "I think she will help make your wish come true."

Kathy brightened considerably and began to laugh, in contrast to her earlier nervousness. "Oh, that would be wonderful!" she exclaimed.

○○○○

Six months later, I visited San Francisco again on business, and decided to call Kathy. She sounded cheerful.

"We bought a house only a month ago. It has a great view of the sea! Come and visit us, you'll love it."

"Congratulations," I replied. "Have you been looking after your mother as I suggested?" She had. Kathy believed her adoptive mother had given her the house, and was unable to hide her joy. A friend had suddenly announced that they urgently wanted to sell, and Kathy was sure, she said, that her mother had arranged it so that a good house would fall into her hands with very little effort.

Dropping her voice, she enquired jokingly, "Do you think she might help me out even more, Mrs. Gibo?"

"Kathy, you mustn't get greedy!" was my reply. "You have to do your bit as well. Whenever you have a drink, even a cup of coffee, remember to pour one for your mother."

"A small price to pay," she replied cheerfully, and said good bye. "And visit us, you'll love it."

MR. BISHOP OF BEVERLY HILLS

Our travels another day took us to Beverly Hills, where the luxurious homes along the way provided a feast for the eyes. Today I was to meet Steven Bishop, singer and songwriter.

Barefooted, Steven came out to greet us on the doorstep, dressed casually in a checkered jacket. Flashing a welcoming smile, he led us into the house. On the wall was a large sculpture in the shape of a record, and our host appeared to have an extensive collection of musical instruments, which he told us he occasionally played.

"I don't believe in spirits at all," he began with a slight smile. "When we die, that's it. No doubt about it." My host appeared determined to have a negative attitude right from the start.

"Well, Steven, just sit down here for us, would you?" I replied. Personally I would rather not have had to deal with someone so skeptical, but when it comes to television work I have little choice. In this case, Steven Bishop had been chosen because he was a friend of the woman coordinating my television appearances.

I began my reading as soon as he sat down on the sofa.

"You had a very lonely childhood, I see."

"Well, I suppose you could say that," was the reluctant reply.

"Your grandmother is here beside you and has started to tell me some things about you. Please listen, won't you?"

"Well, okay, but there could be things I'd rather you didn't say, Mrs. Gibo."

I assured Steven that I would not say anything he didn't want me to, and that in fact my only wish was to find his guardian spirit and give him some advice about how to lead a fulfilling life.

"All right then, go ahead," he said, settling back in his chair.

"First of all," I began, "I see you've had very bad luck with your family relations. You were parted from one parent at a young age."

"Yes, my parents divorced when I was only a kid."

"You didn't live with either of your parents, did you?" I continued.

"No, that's right."

"Your grandmother is telling me all this."

"I remember her very well—she's dead now, mind you."

"In order for you to live happily, I would like you to remember your grandmother and talk to her sometimes. For example, even if you're doing something like sitting down to a meal of say, soup, put some in a small cup and leave it on a table somewhere. Or just think about her, and ask her to look after you, that would do."

"I WAS LONELY FOR A LONG TIME AFTER THAT..."

When I had finished speaking, Steven stood up and went to fetch a photograph.

"This is the only photo I have of my family," he explained. The picture showed Steven, his mother and father, and his

○○○○

younger brother, who was still a baby. The family looked very happy, and the smiling faces gave no indication of the separation to come.

"This photo was taken just before my parents split up," he continued. "They were trying to give the marriage another go, but in the end it didn't work. That was when the loneliness began for me." Steven's eyes fixed on me sadly from behind his rimless glasses.

"Well, you don't have to go into the details, Steven, not while the cameras are rolling. Just don't forget that your grandmother is your guardian spirit: talk to her when you have a problem, ask for her guidance. With her help, the answers will come to you."

Steven nodded his agreement.

As I told him more and more details about his grandmother Steven began to open up to me.

"Has a large dog that you cared for died lately?" I asked.

"Yes...."

"You must remember to say a prayer for the spirit of this dog as well, to enable it to be content."

"I see. I'll definitely give it a try." With this the cameras ceased filming. Steven came over to me and, putting a hand on my shoulder, asked if I would talk to him a little longer. We went into the kitchen.

Not surprisingly he wanted to know what the future held for him, with regard to both his work and his private life.

It was his grandmother who filled in all the details for him, not me. I was only passing on what she wanted her grandson to know.

Steven Bishop's attitude toward me had changed completely. Respectfully he thanked me, promising to do everything I had recommended. He shook my hand warmly, then stood at the door until we were out of sight.

MR. BROWN'S PROBLEM

When I met Mr. Brown, he looked anxious and depressed. His friend Mary, who had accompanied him to the reading, did not

○○○○

waste any time telling me about him. She began talking the moment she sat down.

"Mr. Brown has had no energy at all for about a year now. He used to be very bright and cheery, didn't you?" she said, patting her companion on the shoulder. Mr. Brown was about fifty, but most of his hair was already white, a telltale sign of the man's troubled past. Mary looked just over thirty, and was dressed in gaudy clothing that displayed an incredible lack of taste.

"I got to know Mr. Brown through a friend. I've been racking my brains trying to think of a way to snap him out of his depression, but no luck. I can't stand seeing him like this." Looking into his face, she twisted her brightly painted mouth.

I began as usual, asking my subject to write his name and date of birth. Barely had the words left my mouth when Mary was grabbing his elbow and demanding impatiently, "Come on, write it!"

After this rather abrupt prompting, he did so. His handwriting was excellent.

"Mr. Brown, I believe you are dissatisfied with your job."

"Yes, I really hate my job," he replied.

Mary cut in rudely, "Yes, you might hate it, but you've got to do it."

The woman was starting to seem less like a friend and more like a manager.

"My job really don't suit me, do you know what I mean?" He spoke hesitantly.

"You're some kind of entertainer, aren't you?" I asked. "You perform on stage, like your father, and your grandfather before him. Your grandfather, who is your guardian spirit, told me." I paused. "He's saying you should keep following the family tradition, that you should make use of the talents you have, and if you try doing work other than this, your health will suffer."

Mary interrupted again.

"No, we can't have that," she said hastily. "I don't want him on the stage. I tried to get him a job as an insurance salesman, but that didn't work. Next I got him to train as a jeweler, and that went okay, he studied hard and got qualified. But it didn't last even two years. I asked my cousin to take him on and teach him to sell cars, and that's what he's doing now. Actually that's when he started acting like this, after he went into cars. I've been trying to get him to try harder, but he doesn't have the energy. He's even stopped talking."

Poor Mr. Brown. He seemed to be completely under the thumb of his young girlfriend.

HIS GRANDFATHER'S ADVICE

"Mr. Brown," I began again after the lengthy outburst from the domineering Mary, "your grandfather is telling you to go back to your old job on the stage. He says it's what you do best."

"Really?" he replied, a hint of a smile on his face. "I'm glad, that's taken a load off my mind."

I saw that he would have difficulties with any work that did not involve performing in front of an audience. Unfortunately, the kind of magic act Mr. Brown was trained to perform was becoming increasingly out-of-date, and keeping up with younger performers appeared to be his main worry.

I explained that it was possible to teach an old dog new tricks, as it were, and that he should start studying the latest techniques. It wouldn't be long, I added, before he would be playing to packed houses.

"Do you really think so?" he asked, not entirely convinced. I assured him that it was well within his capabilities, and the pair left, Mr. Brown a great deal happier than he had been when our meeting began.

Some time later, I heard through a friend that Mr. Brown was eager to meet me again. He had quite a story to tell.

After our talk, he had started speaking to his grandfather each night before going to bed, asking the old man to inspire him with a new act.

○○○○

It worked. Appearing in a dream, his guardian spirit described in great detail a trick involving five silk handkerchiefs and a dove. When Mr. Brown performed the trick for a group of friends, it was well received.

Mr. Brown told me that he had never felt more fulfilled by his work than he had been that night. It was hard for him to imagine there had ever been a time when he had not been on the stage, when he had felt like a has-been night after night. It was as if the applause and cheers of that night had restored him to his former glory. No matter how small the venue, magic was his profession, he had decided, and he would never again give it up.

Restored to his former cheerful self, he was a joy to behold.

MRS. MOSE AND HER GRANDMOTHER

A friend of mine once brought a Swiss woman by the name of Mrs. Mose to see me. Her husband was a businessman, and the couple, who lived in Yokohama, got along very well. At that time, however, their close relationship had begun to show signs of strain.

The husband, who had always arrived home from work on the dot of six every night, began spending three nights a week away from home. Mrs. Mose decided to follow him on one such night and saw him meeting two young women.

Her first reaction was amazement, rather than anger or jealousy. She simply could not believe that her husband, who had always been such a serious man, could be having an affair, let alone two.

"I just find it impossible to imagine," she told me. "Even our friends tease us about how much of a perfect couple we are, and say they envy us. It's unbelievable that he could do such a thing."

As she was speaking, a scene appeared before my eye. I saw a farm, with what appeared to be a number of barns and other out-buildings, separated from the house by a tall white fence. An elderly woman of generous build sat in a rocking chair knitting and occasionally gazing out over the farm. She wore a thick grey cardigan. Most of the time her gaze was fixed on the scene before her, except when she turned her attention to the knitting for a moment, examining it over the top of her glasses.

"Mrs. Mose," I said, "I can see a woman knitting, on a farm, and her face is the spitting image of yours."

Mrs. Mose's eyes filled with tears.

"That's my grandmother. My mother died when I was only a child, so I was brought up by my grandmother. Yes, next to the house was a large farm, and that grey cardigan was one she often wore. She loved knitting. She'd sit in the sun all day knitting....I was so lucky to be brought up by her, and yet I hurt her badly." By now the tears were flowing steadily.

"This is my second marriage—and when I was going with my first husband, before we were married, my grandmother warned me about him and opposed the marriage. 'You've been deceived,' she told me. She said he had a very dubious past. We argued, and I slapped her on the face. Afterward I left the house to marry him. She was right about him, though. He spent all my savings and then decided that we should get our hands on my grandmother's money. I was so much under his spell, he managed to persuade me to rob my own home.

"I could have found her most treasured possessions with my eyes closed: afraid that she might die without warning, she had told me exactly where they all were.

"One of the things that meant the most to her was an emerald ring my grandfather had bought her not long after they were married. Every Sunday, she would ask me to fetch the ring from a drawer, and looking at it would tell me stories about my grandfather. He was a good man, who passed away at far too young an age.

"My mother was the only child of the marriage, and my grandmother's only pleasure in life had been watching her grow. After my mother died, she focused all her affection on me.

"After robbing my grandmother of everything she owned, my husband and I stayed together for a while. But once he knew that

〇〇〇〇

there was nothing left to steal, he found another woman and left me. His debts were all that remained of our marriage.

"I never went to apologize to my grandmother. After meeting my present husband, I married again and came to Japan. I wondered how she was, until a friend told me in a letter not long ago that she'd died, all alone, from a heart attack."

I JUST WANT TO MEET MY GRANDDAUGHTER, ONCE

By this time Mrs. Mose was so overwhelmed by her memories that she started to sob uncontrollably. In my vision, her grandmother had been knitting a sweater for her, all the while wanting to see her again. I was almost crying myself.

"The poor woman…" I began again, "even now she's thinking of you, you know. She's letting me know she's there by showing me something she always does. Why don't you take some time off and go back to Switzerland for a while?" I advised. "Visit your grandmother's grave, and apologize to her."

Mrs. Mose took my advice and went back to Switzerland for a visit. On her return to Japan, she gave me some Swiss chocolate, a type that had been a great favorite of her grandmother's.

"Why don't we invite Mrs. Gibo to dinner?" her husband suggested, and I gladly accepted.

When I arrived at their home, preparations had been made for a barbecue. The couple had even gone to the trouble of hanging paper lanterns in the garden. "Hello!" I called, and was greeted by Mrs. Mose, already decked out in an apron and ready to show her cooking skills. The food was delicious, the company pleasant: all-in-all the evening was a most enjoyable one.

When it was time to go, the husband took me aside for a minute.

"Mrs. Gibo," he said quietly, "my wife brought a photo of her grandmother back from Switzerland. When I looked at it, I realized what a terrible thing I had been doing. I think it was the old lady who told me, you know. There'll be no more staying away from home for me."

○○○○

"I should hope not," was my reply. "What on earth do you think you're doing, with a wife as good as this one? Promise me you'll come straight home tomorrow, and every other day."

He agreed, and I left for home, the sound of Mrs. Mose's contented laughter ringing in my ears.

7

CORPORATE GUARDIAN SPIRITS

GUARDIAN SPIRITS HELP COMPANIES GROW

Many people are unaware of the existence of company spirits, which guide those who work within an organization and help it to succeed. A company spirit is that of someone important to the business who has passed away, but who continues to reside at his or her former place of work, watching over it constantly and doing everything possible to steer it toward success.

Like human beings, these spirits have their own personalities. If, for example, the company spirit is that of a patient and cautious person, growth will not be spectacular, and success will be achieved slowly and surely. The spirit of a more impatient individual will cause the company's fortunes to fluctuate sharply over short periods of time. While success may be achieved relatively quickly, pitfalls may appear as suddenly, and without warning.

Thus a company may make rapid progress, or slow. But no matter what stages it passes through in the process of growth in the short term, there can be no doubt that in the long term the presence of a guiding spirit can only be beneficial.

A company's fortunes are greatly influenced therefore by whether it possesses a guardian spirit, and by the character of that spirit. The actual power wielded by a spirit will also be a factor in its effectiveness: if the person to whom the spirit belongs was a natural leader and energetic worker, that spirit will possess enough strength to exert a great deal of influence on the company's fortunes. A more cautious spirit will at times lack the necessary power to do this. Never judge a spirit solely by what appears to be its power, however, as even the weaker ones can contribute to the growth of a company through their tactful advice and careful appraisal of issues.

By now you are probably wondering, can the effectiveness of the company spirit be increased by the living workers within the organization?

It most certainly can be, through the efforts of employees and

oooo

business partners. Even something as simple as a feeling of gratitude toward the spirit felt by all members of an organization can
have considerable effect.

New businesses are often headed by charismatic chief execu-
tives, under whom company employees are united in working toward the success of the organization. Such unity in turn
contributes to strengthening the powers of the company's guardian
spirit. The spirit nurtures the organization, which for its part
strengthens the spirit: thus the laws of give and take operate with
regard to the next world in the same way that they do in this one.

Naturally the identity of their company spirit will be of great
interest to the members of a particular organization. Most probably it will be the guardian spirit of one of the more important people in the company, such as the founder, owner, or a director. It
could also be the guardian spirit of a young person with a bright
future in the company, although this is far less common. In general it is safe to assume that the guardian spirit of the chief executive, or a blood relation, takes on the role of company spirit.

There are those who claim that their guardian spirit is that of a
particular person from the distant past, some well-known historical figure. Such claims should be taken with a very large pinch of
salt. From my own experiences I can say with certainty that a person's guardian spirit is most likely to be a family ancestor of not
more than three generations back.

Company spirits are no exception to this rule. While it is not
actually possible to pinpoint the identity of a company spirit without recourse to the special methods used by psychics, it is almost
certain that it will be the spirit of the chief executive's grandfather
or another forebear who is watching over the company.

Not that it is even necessary to specify the identity of the company's guardian spirit: even without knowing its name, a silent
prayer to "our company spirit" during important meetings in or
out of the office is enough to bring assistance, if the request is
made sincerely.

○○○○

CREATING AN ENVIRONMENT IN WHICH IT IS EASY FOR THE COMPANY SPIRIT TO OPERATE

I believe that the most important factor in the success of a company is the cooperation of all its employees, from the executive level down, in working to the best of their abilities for the organization. A company that conforms to this ideal will become even more successful under the watchful eye of a guardian spirit.

How, then, can a company encourage its guardian spirit to exercise those protective and inspirational powers to the greatest extent possible?

The answer is simple. Employees must create the type of environment in which a spirit feels able to give its very best to the company. I have conducted readings at various companies, and the ones I could confidently predict success for were those in which a spirit could feel at home.

Conversely, when visiting companies that are obviously in decline, I immediately see a number of defects that would make a spirit feel uncomfortable.

If you are serious about wanting your company to prosper and grow, you must work to provide an appropriate environment for your company spirit. Rest assured, there is no need to panic. The company spirit is not going to make great demands of you—it will not, for example, order you to shift your head office to a certain place, or insist that you refurbish your present headquarters. A whispered request along the lines of "Perhaps you could do this for me ..." is as demanding as a spirit will get.

In practical terms, what can be done to create a congenial environment for the company spirit? There are many who will argue that because they can neither hear nor see the spirits, there is no way they can know what their wishes are. This is not the case. Before they departed from this world, spirits were human beings, and in terms of their feelings are almost completely the same as when they were among the living.

Few people can ignore a floor covered in rubbish. No one is

happy if forced to work in a stuffy room with only a small window covered by a curtain.

We all like people who admire us, but we soon come to dislike people who never seem grateful, no matter what we do for them. In other words, if you can see that if the office environment is not conducive to producing good work, or that relations between employees are not going smoothly, then the company spirit can sense the same things and will probably abandon the organization.

What then, can we do to ensure that a company's guardian spirit is happy to devote its energy to helping that company to succeed? Spirits, like us, have their likes and dislikes. The things they enjoyed while alive remain the same even after death. One of the most heartwarming scenes I have witnessed is that of people placing a can of tea on the grave of their grandfather, because he loved to drink it when he was alive. The spirits gain immeasurable satisfaction from such simple actions. Sincerity can never be bought. Standing in front of the person's grave, reciting a silent prayer of thanks to the spirit for its help, and telling it briefly what has been happening at work: all these actions make the spirit feel needed and inspire it to once again do its best for the company.

COMPANY SPIRITS LIKE A CLEAN OFFICE

Just as all spirits find it easier to work when a house is clean and their grave is kept tidy, company spirits function much better when the head office, the axis around which the company's business revolves, is well looked after and pleasant to work in.

Cobwebs on the ceiling, broken windows through which the wind whistles, trash cans that have been left unemptied for a week, stacks of books and documents that look ready to crash at any moment, desks so untidy they can't be distinguished from the neighboring desks, the remains of meals delivered days earlier …given this kind of environment to work in, a spirit will soon become disillusioned and turn its back on the company.

There are those who have no objection to living surrounded by

○○○○

dirt and trash, but no company spirit can stand it. Not surprisingly, they will want to leave as quickly as possible. And when they do, the protection they afford the company against wandering spirits (discontented spirits unable to reach the spirit world who roam the earth) and other types of earthbound spirits will disappear as well, leaving the company vulnerable to the negative influence of these unhappy entities.

All company spirits hate a dirty environment—even the most eccentric. There are no exceptions to this rule.

A business must be well ordered, not only to enable its employees to function easily, but also to ensure that the company spirit feels comfortable enough to stay.

Many companies have ponds or shrubbery on their grounds. If these are looked after, there should be no cause for concern. However, if the water in the pond is dirty, or the shrubs left to wilt, the guardian spirit will be alienated and want to leave. Nor is it a good idea to overstock a pond with fish and other living things. But if you are intent on keeping fish, take the utmost care to ensure their wellbeing. The water must be changed frequently.

In short, cleanliness should be one of the main tenets of the company philosophy.

THE LOBBY: THE "FACE" OF THE COMPANY

When you enter a house in Japan, the first part you see is the *genkan*, or entrance hall. Western homes are much the same in this respect. This is the "face" of the house: when you look at a person, the first thing you take note of is his or her face, and the same goes for a building.

I have been told by spirits that in terms of maintaining a person's fortunes, the entrance of a house is the most important place to keep clean. The same goes for a business. Perhaps it would be best to think of the entrance as the spirit's "office."

It is said that a glance at the entrance to a company's offices will tell you much about the attitude of the employees toward

○○○○

their work and the way they have been trained.

If the entrance does not leave a favorable impression, then the company will never prosper. No matter what the field, a company that has frequent visitors will do well, and an entrance that welcomes those who are arriving is far more inviting than one that fails to do so. An entrance that allows its customers to feel at ease as they pass through is essential if the company is to prosper.

When I conduct a reading at a company, I first stand in the entrance, i.e., the lobby or reception area, close my eyes, and concentrate. The company spirit generally spends most of the day there, working to prevent those who are likely to harm the company from entering and other mishaps from occurring.

So what constitutes a suitable entrance to an office? There are no exact standards. Ease of use, however, would have to be the most important factor, and indeed it is an element of any entrance that is happily occupied by a guardian spirit.

A sense of balance in relation to the rest of the building is also vital. It is difficult to feel relaxed in a lobby that is too large for the building, or, conversely, in one which is too small for the number of visitors that a large company receives every day. An entrance that suits the building it leads into feels comfortable to the company spirit, to employees, and to visitors.

So what should you do if you realize that the entrance to your company's headquarters is too large or too small? If it is too small, with a few alterations it can probably be made larger. The solution is even simpler if it is too large: the creative use of a screen or glass barrier can solve the defect, providing a pleasant change for employees at the same time.

Newspapers often carry stories about employees who jump from their office windows. When this happens, it is important to look carefully at the building, particularly its entrance, and to determine whether the environment is one that is appropriate for the company spirit.

In a publishing company that has handled some of my work

there was an extremely diligent young journalist, a man who seemed quite pleased with his job. But one day, the journalist committed suicide by jumping from an office window.

I had visited the company on business of my own before the incident, and remembered that I had been startled by the appearance of the entrance. It was in such a state of confusion that I found it difficult to discern exactly where I should go in. I spent half an hour wandering around trying to work it out—I had never encountered a building like this. Although it was not so large, it was as confusing to the visitor as a maze, the worst possible kind of entrance to a building.

THE COMPANY SPIRIT IS WATCHING YOU WORK

As I have said, the company spirit, and your own guardian spirit, will assist you where they can. However, for those who think that they can spend their days daydreaming and then ask the spirits to give them a promotion or a salary several times that of their colleagues, I have bad news. If you do this the spirits will abandon you, and there is no greater waste than that.

"I've taken care of the spirits of my ancestors, I've prayed to them diligently every day, and still the company is going downhill—and I've heard rumors of lay-offs, and I know I'm on the list... all this stuff about spirits: maybe they don't really exist, maybe praying is just to give comfort to ourselves...." To anyone thinking along these lines, my advice is: take a close look at your own actions. Perhaps as long as you are praying to your ancestors you feel that all should be well, and perhaps you are forgetting some things you should be doing yourself.

There are of course times when no matter how hard you try you cannot solve a particular problem, but those who rely entirely on the help of the spirits will not get far. Spirits are appalled by the sight of people making no effort to help themselves and counting instead on their ancestors to solve their problems. Praying to and caring for one's ancestors is not enough—you must make your

○○○○

very best effort, or there will be no favorable result. Arriving at work ten minutes early so that you can put your desk in order, devising a detailed schedule in order to use your time more efficiently, reading books to find out more about the world around you, conducting surveys for product development to find out what people really want: through actions like this, diligence and creativity combine to produce results in business.

Working to improve your own performance is as important as prayer in strengthening the company spirit and in ensuring that you and the company are acting in harmony. Such efforts will soon be noticed by both your own guardian spirit and that of the company.

Do not forget: the spirits are always watching you, they cannot be fooled by false promises or actions with no real meaning. They can see your true self, and will decide whether you are worthy of assistance.

LED BY THE PRESIDENT'S GRANDFATHER

ANA (All Nippon Airways) is the world's fifth largest airline in terms of passenger volume, and has grown in leaps and bounds over the last few years, its publicly stated aim being to catch up with and overtake Japan Airlines. Until recently the company was only a domestic airline, but it has attracted attention through its bold ventures into routes between some of the world's major cities.

The spirit guiding the company through this phenomenal growth and with its hands on the actual management of the company is that of the grandfather of Chairman Wakasa Tokuji.

Several other company spirits are working with him. Not all are Japanese: one is British, and this spirit is thought to have played a significant role in the company's venture into international routes.

A large poster displayed behind the reception desk in the lobby is what contributes most to the environment of the company, which is conducive to hard work and the enjoyment of that work. The company spirit likes this poster and thinks when it looks at it, "I must make this business an even bigger one, a more diverse one, I must do whatever I can to help it achieve success." ANA's lobby is an excellent example of one where the interior matches exactly the preferences of the company spirit.

The lobby is unfortunately a little dark, and this I believe is its only fault. I suspect this was a factor in earlier troubles that the company experienced, but from which it appears to be recovering.

I think this company spirit was a man who had looked up at the blue skies and wanted to be in them from the time he was a boy, and that is why the predominant color in the company, from fittings to uniforms, is the same light blue as the sky. This choice of a particular color has helped ANA to leap ahead, as it has helped several other companies.

As I have been thinking about this company, a blue and white scarf with diagonal stripes, moving through the air, has appeared before me. The fact that it has appeared after I have been talking about the company spirit indicates that the spirit would like the company to introduce this type of scarf for its stewards and stewardesses. There is no doubt that if ANA answers this request, it will become even more successful.

ITO'S GUARDIAN SPIRIT IS ITS FOUNDER

The Ito Trading Company, which started in Osaka as a textile trading company, has been improving its performance steadily over the years. Its prospects in the growing field of communications are excellent, thanks to the company's guardian spirit, its founder Ito Chubei.

Ito was a very precise man who believed in getting things right down to the last detail. For this reason his spirit seldom stays for long in one section of the company. One minute he may be in the boardroom, the next at the door giving his blessing to salespeople leaving the office. His determination and vitality have served to

○○○○

build a solid foundation for the company's activities.

According to my reading, this is a company that, sending its best employees out into new fields, is forming a number of subsidiary organizations. Employees are receiving advice from the company spirit concerning new business opportunities in the fields of energy and communications. Those employees who have been so advised receive a flash of inspiration, a new idea which had never occurred to them before.

BRIDGESTONE'S GUARDIAN SPIRIT, ISHIBASHI SHOJIRO

Bridgestone is one of the world's top three tire manufacturers. While its business is centered on tire and tube production, other manufactured goods and sports-related products make up a growing percentage of sales, presently around eighteen percent, and the company is also involved in land development. Standing in front of the Bridgestone headquarters in the center of Tokyo, I was struck immediately by the energy emanating from the land on which the building stands.

As I had suspected, the company spirit was that of Ishibashi Shojiro. It was he who influenced company directors in their decision to purchase this particular piece of land. From my reading I understood that Ishibashi was a quintessential businessman who liked to build a solid foundation before he embarked on a business venture.

One would expect that a company with a guardian spirit of this type would be basically cautious in its business dealings, that it would count contributing to the welfare of society through the production of high-quality goods among its aims, and that it would take the utmost care over quality control.

Rather than being reluctant to embark on new ventures, however, Bridgestone has recently moved into a number of fields far removed from its traditional one of tire manufacture—from golf balls and sports equipment to building materials and even robots.

The choice of Bridgestone's headquarters can only have been

○○○○

inspired by Ishibashi's spirit. Easy to find and centrally located for customer convenience, it reflects Ishibashi's shrewd calculation—there is no doubt that he was a salesman first and foremost. Furthermore, he had always been interested in property.

As the example of Bridgestone shows, a company's guardian spirit works best in those areas of the business in which the person had a special interest, or in which he or she was particularly knowledgeable. These are the areas in which the business will show the most promise.

AMERICAN SPIRITS IN MACDONALD'S

MacDonald's—the name is synonymous with hamburgers. The guardian spirits working for MacDonald's Japan are Dick and Mack, founders of the world-famous fast-food chain.

As children the brothers were poor, and everything they owned was earned the hard way. On one occasion they saved up for a long time to buy a red bicycle, and I believe that experience was part of what inspired them to found the now-famous hamburger chain in their later years.

My readings have shown me that the two brothers are still riding their red bicycle, traveling around the Japanese branches of MacDonalds to give advice and assistance to employees.

Red is their favorite color. As is evident from a visit to any MacDonalds, the color dominates the interior of every franchise.

Dick and Mack believed in trying to step into their customers' shoes, and this attitude is reflected in that of their company's employees. Company president Fujita Den is well-known as a man who never neglects to say thank you to every customer.

There is no doubt in my mind that the sincerity and attention to detail of MacDonalds' company spirits will ensure a bright future for the business.

WHO WATCHES A CERTAIN PUBLISHER IN GINZA?

I visited this company on an assignment for a magazine. As I sat in the visitors' room, casually taking in the interior of the office, a group of ten desks to the right of me suddenly appeared to darken. Startled, I fixed my eyes on them, and as I did, a man dressed in what appeared to be the uniform of a security guard materialized and began to walk among the desks.

It was two in the afternoon, hardly the usual time for a security guard to be patrolling. Perhaps this company did things a little differently from others, I thought as I watched him.

To my surprise, the figure pulled out a flashlight and shone it on each of the desks. Aged about sixty with a round, pleasant-looking face, he seemed to be taking his work very seriously.

Eventually, the chief editor arrived, and we completed our business. He had something else on his mind as well, however.

"By the way, Mrs. Gibo, I'd like to ask you about some strange goings-on here … some of the staff say they've seen a ghost in the offices. We have a room with three beds that employees use when they need to stay over, and several people say they've seen a man with a flashlight standing by the middle bed," he explained. "And those desks over there," he continued, pointing at the row that had been in darkness earlier, "belong to the staff of one of our magazines. No matter how hard they work, magazine sales are down, and they're all very depressed about the situation."

I asked to be shown to the room with the three beds.

As I stood beside the middle bed, the sound of someone walking reached my left ear. The footsteps were those of a man, and they stopped beside the middle bed. I felt a flashlight shining on me and looked up into the face of its bearer. I saw at once that it was a spirit, the security guard I had seen earlier.

"And who are you?" I enquired.

IN A SECOND, THE SURROUNDINGS CHANGED
As I spoke, the surroundings changed in an instant. This prime area in the center of Tokyo, crowded with tall buildings, was transformed into a desolate place with long grass waving in the

○○○○

wind. I could see a single building, looking very much like a temporary affair, inside of which sat a row of men at desks.

I realized at once that the spirit was showing me how the company had begun. "It would be better if you didn't work on men's magazines at those desks," he advised. "Please tell them to work on magazines for young women there. I know I'm right about this: I've been here, walking around and making sure that everything's in order, since the company was what you see before you."

I told the editor what I had seen and heard. Surprised, he replied that a story about a security guard who had been with the company till his death, and whose only concern seemed to be for its welfare, had been passed down from one editor to another.

"Okay, so men's magazines are no good there...well, we'll have to take a chance and try doing something in the way of a magazine for young women instead."

He thanked me for my advice, and we parted. I remember it was a scorching hot day in August.

Some years later, I received a call from the editor.

"Mrs. Gibo, thank you for your assistance," he began. "Do you remember...you advised us to switch from a men's magazine to one for young women in a certain section?"

I said that I remembered, and conjured up an image in my mind of the company's head office near the Kabukiza theater.

"We changed direction soon after that, and sales of the new magazine have gone through the roof," he continued excitedly. I asked what the name of the new magazine was.

Hanako, was the reply. *Hanako* is Japan's top-selling magazine for young women, the one they buy in order to find out about the latest trends.

8
THE AFTERLIFE

MY BRUSH WITH DEATH AT THE AGE OF TWENTY-ONE

I'd like to go back now to a bleak day in early January of my twenty-first year. I remember grey clouds filling the winter sky, and icy sleet falling on and off all day.

On waking I felt terribly ill, and, thinking that I would prefer to stay in bed for the day, I got up and took some medicine we had in the house. My mother looked anxiously at my face and remarked that I was very pale.

"Yes, I do feel a bit cold," I replied.

I had never been very healthy, and my mother was accustomed to assessing how I was by looking at my face in the morning.

"I've got a bit of a headache, but I'm all right really," I continued, forcing a smile to allay her fears. Despite my best efforts, however, I began to feel even worse, and after a couple of hours actually started having trouble breathing. Finding myself unable to stay up, I crawled back into the warm futon, thinking I would be all right if I stayed there. No sooner had I got in, however, when my shoulders started to shake uncontrollably in a violent chill. My mother, sick with worry, drew the futon up to my shoulders and put her hand on my forehead. Startled by the intensity of my fever, she called the family doctor.

I could hear my mother's voice, but it seemed far away, as I felt myself slipping into unconsciousness. I willed my heavy eyelids open and stared blankly at the snow outside through a clear section at the top of the frosted-glass door.

Next to my pillow was a hibachi for heating the room. In it sat a small bowl of water that was rapidly turning to steam. So fierce was the heat that I thought I could smell the bowl beginning to melt.

Even in my drowsy state I could feel my chest beginning to hurt and understood that my condition was worsening. Eventually my eyes refused to stay open. The instant they closed I was overwhelmed by a sensation of being dragged down into the ground. It was as if I had sunk eight or twelve inches into the

oooo

floor. At the same time my breathing seemed to become easier, and I felt a heavy weight pressing on the back of my head. Suddenly I was floating in the air and looking down on my body, sunken into the floor.

I remember that instant when there were two of me very well. I felt as if I were being drawn up by some force and attached to the ceiling by suction.

I saw my mother, her face creased with worry, and the doctor who had rushed to my side, sitting by me.

My father was there as well. He had not been at home when I first crawled into my futon feeling ill, but had appeared in the meantime and now kneeled beside me, his face tense with anxiety as he watched the doctor completing his examination.

"My parents are worried," I remember thinking, "but I'm up here by the ceiling...I wonder why."

I LEFT, FLOATING OUT OF THE ROOM

It was an incredible feeling. The pain was gone, as was the chill that had set my body shivering.

Outside my room was the hall, and, pulling aside the sliding door which separated the two, I floated out. Compared with my room, the hallway was cold and uninviting, but I steered myself out and toward the front door.

Just as when you dive underwater your body keeps wanting to float to the surface, so it was with me in the air. With great effort I managed to fight my buoyancy and come down to stand on my own two feet, although I still felt extremely light.

I had been a sensitive child who hated touching insects with my bare hands, or very smooth paper. Touching cold glass had also been one of the things I loathed, and when I opened the glass door I was always careful to touch only the crosspiece, about an inch wide, which was part of the latticework on the door, and not the glass itself. I used the same method on this occasion.

○○○○

The door opened easily, and beyond it was a scene which took my breath away.

My brother was standing there, the brother who had been killed in the war, the brother who had always taken care of me, the brother who had said little and studied a lot, the brother nine years older than me.

His expression was somewhat out of character, however: cold and unfriendly. For a second I thought I was mistaken.

"Come on, let's go," he said.

Nodding silently, I went to follow him. It was then that I noticed he had someone with him, a woman. It was my cousin, who had died suddenly at the age of fifteen. Because we had lived far from each other, I had only met her once or twice. It never occurred to me to wonder why she was with my brother, whom she could hardly have known.

The road we walked along was of damp red earth, and as we left the house, a view completely different from the one to which I was accustomed spread before me. The earth felt good to walk on, with no gravel or rubbish underfoot, and a gentle breeze was blowing.

It felt like May, when the trees are covered with spring growth. The temperature was comfortable, the breeze pleasant. Walking happily along as I was doing, I failed to notice for some time that my brother and cousin had disappeared. When I did notice there seemed no cause for concern: somehow I just knew where to walk.

Before I had gone much farther, I noticed a field of large white chrysanthemums flowering just off the road. Looking at them, I continued to walk. My legs, oddly enough, were not feeling the least bit tired.

A few minutes later I reached the bank of a river. Judging from the speed of the water's flow it was not that deep, but it must have been about six yards across. I was overwhelmed by a desire to cross it—on the other side I could see a string of low hills, devoid

○○○○

of vegetation, and I found myself wanting to climb them.

SOMEONE FROM THE PAST ACROSS THE RIVER

To cross that river, however, I would have to take off my shoes, and my clothing would probably get wet. I was still hesitating when I spotted someone I knew over on the other side. It was my brother Masao, who had died in a car accident at the age of fifteen.

He was calling out to me, but I was unable to hear a word. Then he started signaling, and it soon became obvious he was telling me not to cross the river. I ignored him, however, and began to cross.

Lifting my skirt I started to put my feet in the water, then glanced up at my brother again. He was watching me, with tears running down his cheeks. When I saw his tears I realized I really ought not to be crossing the river, and turned back. As I did I heard my mother's voice, first in the distance, then gradually louder and louder.

"Aiko, don't give up," she was shouting, over and over. With an effort I opened my eyes, to see her face in front of mine. She too was crying. As I watched, however, her expression changed to one of joy.

"She heard me at last!" she cried, and beside her I saw my father and the doctor, both smiling with relief.

"She should be stable now, but I'll come back in about three hours to check." So saying, the doctor got slowly up and walked out toward the front door. By now I was able to take in the surroundings quite easily.

I could still see snowflakes drifting gently down, and smell the bowl in the brazier. My mother clasped my hand and clung to it for what seemed like forever.

This was my experience of the afterworld, and even now I can vividly recall every detail of every scene.

A single white chrysanthemum decorated the family altar in our house at that time, and as I looked at it, I realized to my

OOOO

surprise that it was this exact same flower which I had seen reproduced many times by the side of that road of red earth.

THE TRUTH ABOUT THE SPIRIT WORLD

Often when I am absorbed in a problem, or just thinking about nothing in particular, my younger brother appears before me and talks to me about the spirit world.

He sits in front of me as if he were alive, so I ask him questions just as I would of a living person. Like everyone else, I want to know the truth about the spirit world.

"What sort of a place is it? Are there other people there? What is the weather like? Are there animals too?" I fire questions at him, but he never seems to find it tiresome, and answers each one patiently.

His personality is the same as when he was alive: always glad to help, he never made anyone feel that they were a nuisance.

As a child, Masao loved to keep pigeons. He studied their habits and seemed to be able to communicate with them. Although only a child, he was well respected for his skills in this field, and pigeon enthusiasts often gathered at our home to consult him about the feeding and treatment of their birds.

Masao's love of birds was not confined to pigeons. He even had a soft spot for the chickens that roamed our backyard. Chickens are said to be rather unfriendly toward humans, but where my brother was concerned it was a different matter. When he was due home from school, the chickens would gather round the front door and wait for him to arrive.

Masao really was one of the kindest people I have ever had the good fortune to know. No matter what the question, and no matter who asked it, his replies were always patient and precise. Now he has traveled to the spirit world, but this aspect of his personality remains unchanged.

My more detailed knowledge of the spirits has come not from extensive study nor from any famous priest, but from what my brother has told me.

○○○○

When I was a child, the messages I received intermittently from my brother were naturally of great interest, but I never thought to write them down or tell others about them. Despite this they have remained in my memory, each one as fresh as the day I heard it.

Piecing together what he has told me, I have come to the conclusion that the world we arrive in after death is not nearly as vibrant and interesting as the one in which we live. Its colors are muted, and the mode of thought of its inhabitants is also quite different from that of the living.

Life is not always easy by any means: there are times when we have to study hard, and times when we make mistakes and learn from them. But for most of us, life brings joy as well as sorrow and pain, and there are some activities we would not give up for the world: enjoying a favorite piece of music, appreciating the work of a skilled artist, and spending time with our friends, to name but a few.

All these are pleasures of this world, but not of the next—they do not exist in the afterworld. Instead the spirits spend their hours trudging wearily along what can be a very monotonous road, with the hope of achieving reincarnation. Their existence has none of the highs and lows that we, the living, experience from day to day.

A FLOWER TO EASE THE BURDEN OF THE SPIRITS

So far I have emphasized the importance of taking care of the spirits of our loved ones, the reason being that even a single flower blooming along the road they are traveling, or a kind thought from their family, will enliven the journey I have described. The spirits are far more conscious of the communication that takes place between souls, whether of the living or the dead, than we are, and nothing pleases them more than being remembered in some way.

Earlier I spoke of my own experience with the afterworld, and you may remember the white chrysanthemums blooming alongside the road, and the fact that they were identical to those sitting

○○○○

on our family altar, even down to the number of leaves. If you decorate the road on which the spirits walk in this way, it will cease to be monotonous for them. Even a single flower placed in a glass will, for that spirit, become a field of blooms stretching over a vast area.

Flowers have a pleasant scent and are a pleasure to the eye, so for the spirits of people who loved flowers, an offering of one of their favorite blossoms will make them happier than anything else you could give them. What more could such spirits desire than a carpet of their favorite flowers covering their path through the afterworld?

When you make such an offering, while saying the name of the person for whom it is intended, the spirit of that person will join you, and enjoy the sight and smell of the flower, multiplied many times down the path through the spirit world.

Some people believe that because roses have thorns they are not suitable for such offerings—but in fact as long as the thorns are removed there is no reason why they cannot be used.

All flowers have the power to please. There is no one, in this world or the next, who can frown or complain when faced with flowers.

The belief many people have that there is nothing after death is naturally that which saddens the spirits the most. The demise of the body does not equal that of the soul, which lives forever.

My brother often comes to me with a request of the following nature:

"Aiko, I'm worried about the Suzukis' grandmother... she loved tea so much when she was alive, but her family has never given her any since she came here, not even once. Mother always leaves cake out for me when everyone has some, and tells me to eat it, so I never miss out. Can't you get the Suzukis to do the same thing for their grandmother, and give her a cup of tea from time to time?"

Sometimes I receive such requests from him several times a day.

○○○○

MRS. YAMAMOTO AND THE KIND GRANDMOTHER

I remember a girl I knew as a child, by the name of Yamamoto, who was the apple of her grandmother's eye. Wherever she went the old lady would follow, never once missing a sports day or a school festival in which her granddaughter was taking part.

Often the grandmother would make the girl's favorite sushi, which contained cucumber, and take it to school for her. The child was a fussy eater, so it was mainly thanks to the efforts of her grandmother that she managed to grow up without even catching a cold.

The old lady died when Mrs. Yamamoto was at junior high school. Many years later, the same little girl, now grown up, was in bed with a raging fever when her grandmother appeared to her in a dream. Placing her hand on the younger woman's forehead, she whispered, "We'll soon have that fever down."

Waking with a start, Mrs. Yamamoto promised out loud to her grandmother that if she helped her to recover, she would make the cucumber sushi the old lady had made for her years ago. Unfortunately, once she had recovered, Mrs. Yamamoto forgot her promise. Some time later, I met her in the street.

Beside her I could see an elderly lady. Surprised, I took a closer look. Yes, there was no doubt about it. As I watched, she took a roll of cucumber sushi and, placing it on a plate, offered it to me silently.

"Mrs. Yamamoto, there is an old lady holding some cucumber sushi standing next to you," I informed my companion. Her face turned white as a sheet.

"Cucumber sushi you say? I always meant to make some, but in the end never got around to it." She told me about her dream.

"Mrs. Yamamoto, I'd advise you to make some very soon," I said, and I have no doubt that she did.

THE OLD LADY APPEARS AGAIN IN HER DREAMS

A few days later, Mrs. Yamamoto's grandmother appeared again in her dreams, this time holding a roll of cucumber sushi and

○○○○

looking very happy. Two days after this, while Mrs. Yamamoto was traveling with some friends, a very strange thing happened.

They were having dinner in their hotel, and Mrs. Yamamoto was just about to start eating the fish that had been prepared for them when suddenly she found herself not wanting to touch it.

The other two ate it all, including her portion, all the while remarking how delicious it was. A few hours later, however, they both felt horribly ill. Mrs. Yamamoto alone managed to escape food poisoning.

There is no doubt that Mrs. Yamamoto, who loved fish and would usually have eaten more of it than her two friends, was helped by her grandmother that day, as an expression of the old lady's gratitude for the sushi. Mrs. Yamamoto herself realized this.

Mrs. Yamamoto's experience is an excellent example of how even such a small gesture as preparing food for the spirit of a departed loved one can protect us from harm which might otherwise befall us.

Caring for the spirits means showing by your actions that your heart is with them. Talking to the spirit, even if just in your heart, is another excellent way of showing you care. Thanking them for their help, telling them what you have done during the day—nothing makes them happier than being spoken to.

As we progress along the path of life, our ancestors walk along the path of the spirit world. If we help each other, pain need not exist in either of our worlds, and both will become much better places.

SUICIDE

Far too many people commit suicide because they have come to hate the world for some reason and they want to disappear from it. My brother, however, tells me that suicide is the one action a person should never contemplate, no matter how unhappy they are.

○○○○

People are driven to suicide in order to escape from mental or physical pain. What they should realize, however, is that this pain returns to plague them again and again even after they have passed into the spirit world.

Our universe consists of a large number of diverse living things: humans, animals, and plants, and the life span of each individual organism is already decided at birth.

How is it decided? Through the process of reincarnation. Our life span in this world is dependent on our actions in the last. Living out our lives in this world to their predestined length is the natural way to do things, and we will be happiest by if we follow this way.

Suicide, therefore, by cutting off a life before its term is complete, defies the natural order of things. The spirit of someone who has taken his or her own life realizes soon after it enters the afterworld that it will pay for choosing to die by experiencing even more pain than before. Suicide, then, is something to be avoided, no matter what trials you are going through in life.

We all know people to whom this advice was never given, or who ignored it. We can still help to ease their burden—as the living, it is our duty.

The spirit of a person who has committed suicide may even let us know they want help by making life difficult for us. Let me explain the reason for this.

In general, human beings, when their lives are going smoothly, have little or no thought for those who have already left this world . It is only when things begin to go wrong that they start to think their ill-fortune might have something to do with the spirits. Please, do not forget about these poor wandering spirits whose only means of getting the attention they desperately need is by causing harm to the living.

HOMES WHERE A PLACE-BOUND SPIRIT RESIDES
I am sure you have heard the expressions "place-bound spirit"

○○○○

and "floating spirit" before. A place-bound spirit is most commonly lingering near the place where the person concerned died.

It could be there for any one of a number of reasons. One of the most tragic scenarios, however, is when a person works all his or her life to buy a house, then is cheated out of it and hounded to an early grave. That person's spirit will more often than not remain in the house, unable to leave.

Such people literally "carry their regrets beyond the grave," as the saying goes. Their attachment to their home is every bit as strong as when they were alive. Attachment as strong as this is by no means restricted to houses—walking in the mountains in autumn, I sometimes encounter the spirits of hikers who were killed there. They remain tied to the place that changed their destinies.

All over the world people tell stories about "haunted houses" and "mystery spots." Such places are inhabited by place-bound spirits. Some years ago, I encountered one such spirit while visiting Czechoslovakia. About fifteen minutes from the hotel for foreign travelers I was staying in was a famous Jewish cemetery. As I was walking by one evening, I spied a gravestone which looked as if it was going to fall over any minute. What startled me more, however, was what was standing behind it.

It was a man. But when I took a closer look at his face, the horror of what I saw rooted me to the spot. His eyes were missing, and in their place there remained only two gaping sockets.

I concentrated hard. It was beginning to get dark, so perhaps I had been mistaken. But no—the man without eyes remained there for a minute or so before disappearing.

The cemetery was closed at night, and there was no way anyone could have entered. There was only one explanation for the presence of the man: he was a place-bound spirit, doomed to linger in the cemetery instead of passing properly into the afterworld. My heart ached with sympathy for his plight.

Not all place-bound spirits are as wretched as this. People who love the place they were born and raised in can also stay on earth

ОООО

and linger there. Even though they have passed away, they continue to think only of the welfare of their former home and can in fact contribute significantly to its prosperity.

When spirits remain place-bound because they have taken their own life, however, they will be so tortured by remorse that there is no way they can conceivably contribute to the welfare of the area they once lived in.

These spirits remain on earth in the hope that if they are here, perhaps they will be able to return to life, knowing all the while that this wish will never be fulfilled. Their remorse over taking their own lives will ensure that they remain torn between this world and the next, never content.

Spirits may also remain in a place where they as persons accomplished some great achievements. They want to have these memories close at hand. Spirits of this type which I have encountered have a completely different expression from that of suicide victims. Suffused with the memories of their past, they glow with contentment.

PEOPLE'S CHARACTERS DON'T CHANGE AFTER DEATH

The differences between the place-bound spirit of someone who has committed suicide and that of someone who has performed some deed of note are great, but the two types of spirit do have one thing in common: no matter what their reason for remaining on earth, their personalities remain the same as when they were alive.

People who do not let themselves be concerned about matters of little importance or who recover quickly from setbacks generally proceed smoothly into the afterlife. People who take their own lives, on the other hand, generally do it because they have become so preoccupied with their problems that they see no other way out of them.

The majority of place-bound spirits are therefore people who have committed suicide, remaining eternally obsessed with their

OOOO

own mode of death, and regretting that they ever chose to give up on life. People who take great interest in the affairs of others, and people full of nervous energy, often appear before me after death as floating spirits. My brother was a hard-working and serious boy, often prompting our mother to remark that he always seemed to be on the move. This aspect of his personality remained unchanged even after his death.

He comes to me not only when I speak to him, but at other times as well, even when I have not been thinking about him. Before I know it he is gone again: he never was one to waste time, and death has not changed this.

Thanks to my contact with spirits, I can say with certainty that a person retains the same personality even after death. This personality will remain the same during the whole of the period in which the spirit is striving for reincarnation.

We all know people who worry unnecessarily about the most trifling matters, and these people also remain the same after death. Anxiety about their families fills their every moment, and they often become floating spirits, watching over their loved-ones' every move.

The most important thing to remember about all these spirits remaining on earth is that if the family they have left behind speaks to them, they will feel more at ease, and come to understand that their place is in the spirit world, not in the world of the living.

Even the wretched spirits of people who have committed suicide can receive great comfort from the actions of friends and family. But simply thinking of the deceased when they are gathered together, perhaps sharing a cup of tea or coffee with the deceased's spirit, they will lighten the spirit's burden of regret and enable it to begin leaving this world to progress to the next.

FAME AND FORTUNE MEAN NOTHING IN THE SPIRIT WORLD

Hard-earned possessions and worldly fame mean nothing in the

○○○○

afterworld. Rich or poor, everyone is equal.

Many Japanese believe that buying a posthumous name from a Buddhist temple will increase their chances for a happy afterlife. This belief is strong enough to persuade many people to pay temples great sums of money for the privilege.

The wealthy may be able to buy such a name, regardless of what kind of life they have led or how they have hurt others. But in reality posthumous names serve only to satisfy the egos of the living. Thinking that a posthumous name will guarantee great influence in the spirit world is a grave mistake.

How can I be so certain? Quite simply, from what the spirits have told me over the years about themselves.

Posthumous names are not used in the spirit world. There are people able to buy fame and position quite easily in this world, but knowing something of the spirits, I would have been surprised if this purchased status were to extend to the afterlife. I was relieved when a number of them assured me that we are all equal after death.

Among the wealthy there are those who have built their fortunes by scrimping and saving: never eating good food, never traveling...just working. This is not the sort of life a person should lead. I am not suggesting that I believe in profligate spending and avoiding work, but we should at least have a few small pleasures to indulge in from time to time. As the saying goes, "you can't take it with you." Nothing could be truer.

DO HEAVEN AND HELL REALLY EXIST?

Many believe the afterworld is divided into heaven and hell. "Heaven" we often imagine to be as we have seen it in paintings: a peaceful place where ethereal music is played. "Hell," according to many artists, is where snakes writhe amid pools of blood.

These images are part of the lesson many of us had hammered into us in our childhood—if we do bad things we will go to hell, and if we behave we will go to heaven, led by angels to the accompaniment of music. This is what our parents told us.

As a means of inculcating certain values into children, these are marvelous stories. As a simple and effective way of teaching us to strive for good rather than evil from an early age, I believe they have a role to play.

However, as a psychic, I know the true nature of heaven and hell, from what the spirits have told me. My brother described hell to me in the following manner.

When we leave this world, all of us travel the same road, whether we have led good lives or immoral ones. All of us trudge along that path of damp red earth. As we do, some of us will think, "I've done everything I should have. I've lived a virtuous life. I've left the world behind now, with no regrets. All I have to do now is walk toward the next world.

"My friends and family have not forgotten me. They talk to me, they leave my favorite food out for me, and whenever they gather together, they mention my name. When I think of their love, I know that the best thing for me to do is to travel toward the next world. I also know that while I walk I can enjoy the sight and scent of the flowers that they send to me."

Spirits able to think such pleasant thoughts as these are the ones that we can say are in heaven.

SOULS WHO WALK THROUGH THE AFTERLIFE FILLED WITH REGRET

What of those that are dissatisfied with the circumstances of their death, and those who cannot accept that they are no longer among the living?

"I was driving too fast. If I hadn't been in such a hurry, I wouldn't have had to die before my time was up."

"That person killed me before I was ready for the spirit world ....It's not fair, I don't care what the circumstances are, I don't want to walk through the afterworld yet."

There is no end of reasons why a person may not be satisfied

oooo

with his or her death. By far the most common, however, is suicide.

"If I had just changed my life, or used a different method to do what I did, I could have got out of the situation I was in and not have had to die. And to make things worse, my family won't even offer me a flower or two, let alone visit my grave. They've forgotten me as if I never existed. I want to go back so much…and try again. I know I could get it right next time."

Spirits tormented by such thoughts as they travel through the afterworld could be said to be in hell. Forgetting, as the expression goes, "all worldly desires", and one's own history, and becoming a spirit able to walk through the afterworld with no regrets is the only way to escape from this self-imposed purgatory.

What constitutes "heaven" or "hell" therefore depends on how the spirit feels as it walks through the afterworld.

Fortunately those spirits walking through a Hell of their own creation are not necessarily doomed to do so forever. With the help of the living, Hell can become Heaven. Of course those who while on earth committed heinous crimes such as murder, or who cheated someone out of property or otherwise hurt another person deeply, may find that their families do not want to send them love, making their journey through the afterworld more difficult still.

The road to that part of the afterworld known as heaven is long, and the numerous regrets weighing on the minds of many spirits can make the journey a difficult one. Wrongdoing brushed aside as being of no great importance while we are alive is not so simple to sweep under the carpet after death.

IN THE AFTERWORLD, ONLY THE SPIRITUAL EXISTS

Our daily lives are filled with our work, our hobbies, and a thousand and one other things. Matters soon forgotten in the rush of everyday existence, however, may take on overwhelming importance in the afterworld.

As I have mentioned, walking through the spirit world bearing

○○○○

the burdens of ill-feeling and remorse is in itself a kind of hell, because the afterlife is a place where we relive the pain of our lives. This process could be most accurately described as a type of discipline for our souls.

Here I must point out that peoples' attitudes toward some things are different after they have left this world from what they were when they were alive.

Perhaps they neglected to give up their seat to a handicapped person, or borrowed money from a friend without repaying it, or ignored the troubles of an acquaintance. Such events may have taken place many years previously and at the time may have seemed to be of little significance, but once people enter the spirit world they are reminded vividly of all such episodes and must make amends to the person concerned in their own way.

In this world we may enjoy beautiful scenery, listen to and appreciate music, desire certain objects. The material aspect of our lives has a great influence on our feelings. In the afterworld, however, only spiritual matters are of importance.

The most satisfying walk through the afterworld for a spirit is that which, through freedom from worldly passions and desires, leads in a straight line toward reincarnation. Supporting the spirit as it travels along this path is the duty of the living. Cooperation between those who walk in this world and those who walk in the next is, I believe, the key to happiness for us all.

○○○○

9

TRANSMIGRATION AND REINCARNATION

MY VIEW OF REINCARNATION

How is the afterworld organized? The spirits tell me the following. When individuals' lives have come to an end, they begin walking, alone, along the long path of the afterworld. This path is unchanging: incredibly, however, all of the spirits traveling on it know exactly where they are going. It is as if some internal force were guiding them step by step.

There are spirits who directly after death feel a great longing for the world they have left, and some who do not even realize they have left it.

Eventually, however, they begin to walk, lost deep in their memories of the world of the living. At this stage they are still not long in the afterworld, and their mode of thought is much the same as when they were alive.

As they walk further on, the surroundings begin to change. The movement of the wind is different, the light becomes dimmer. The troubles that plagued them while they were among the living begin to be shed one by one, like layers of clothing. This is how those who have fulfilled all their obligations and carried out the duties required of them while alive progress through the afterworld.

As the spirit walks on even further, its thoughts gradually begin turning to reincarnation. When the long journey is over, the spirit will emerge into a dazzling light, as if from a tunnel. With this, the spirit has arrived at the place where it will be reincarnated as another human being. I call this period from the spirit's entrance into the afterworld to its eventual rebirth as another human being "transmigration and reincarnation."

It is important that a spirit be able to walk with confidence toward a new life, rather than trudging slowly forever along that monotonous red-earth road. By letting the deceased know of our love for them and our determination not to forget them, we encourage them on their journey.

Reincarnation is an aspect of the spirit world which cannot be

oooo

overlooked in any study of what happens after death. Here I would like to explore the topic a little further.

AN INCREDIBLE TALE OF REINCARNATION

Once again this is a story from my childhood and concerns events which took place when I went to visit relatives in Chiba prefecture. The trains were infrequent and uncomfortable, belching out clouds of black smoke, but I always looked forward with excitement to a trip to my grandmother's house.

Street lights were a rarity then; instead, the summer nights were lit up by fireflies, which glowed like thousands of tiny lightbulbs.

Catching these fireflies was one of my greatest pleasures, as was gathering mushrooms, sometimes so thick on the ground that you were forever squashing them unintentionally with your feet. The forest was something quite different from what I was used to, and I loved it. As a child who never spoke, this interaction with nature was something I could truly enjoy.

I was staying at my grandmother's when something I will never forget happened in the village. A family living there had a two-year-old son, a sickly child unable even to utter a sound. One day the little boy caught a cold, which rapidly developed into pneumonia, from which he died. After he died, his mischievous older brother wrote the child's name on one of the child's own tiny plump hands; it stayed there while the hands were placed in an attitude of prayer, and the child was buried in the family grave.

More than ten years passed. The older brother grew up and got married, and his wife gave birth to a child. The house was soon in an uproar—one of the child's hands was clenched tightly and would not open. Taking the baby's hand in her own, the baby's grandmother opened it out one finger at a time, praying as she did. When she had finished, the family gasped at what they saw. On the child's hand were the same characters that its father had written on the hand of his dead baby brother.

○○○○

It goes without saying that the story soon spread around the village. I heard that the family took some earth from the other child's grave and tried to rub the name off with it, but I don't know for sure what happened after they did that. The baby bore no physical resemblance to his father's younger brother, and unlike him was a fast learner. There is no doubt in my mind, however, that he was a reincarnation of the child who would, had he lived, have grown up to be his uncle.

PROVIDENCE AND REINCARNATION

Although people are reincarnated, they never have the same appearance or personality as they did in their previous lives. If they had striven to master a particular trade or other skill and had not succeeded, however, they may be reincarnated with the talent they were not blessed with in their previous life. What we know as natural or inborn talent is a result of this process.

The spirits tell me also that members of the same family: parents, brothers and sisters, husbands, wives, and children, have often been related to each other in previous lives. Family members, however, could have been living as a family anywhere on earth, not necessarily in the country in which they share their present life.

Incredible as it may seem, we may have been a member of a completely different racial or national group in any one or all of our previous lives. What better reason could there be for doing away with war than this?

What can be said with certainty regarding reincarnation is that we will most likely come back as another human being, and of the same sex. I believe that the way we act in this lifetime has great influence on our happiness in the next, because I know that if we work to please our guardian spirit in this life, it, and the other spirits, will guide us toward contentment in our new life.

To those unfortunate people who have lost a brother or sister or a young child I say: pray to your guardian spirit to ensure that

OOOO

its next life is long and fulfilling. This is what looking after the spirits is all about.

OOOO

10

TAKING CARE OF
THE SPIRITS

NO MATTER WHAT YOUR RELIGIOUS BELIEFS, YOU CAN LOOK AFTER YOUR ANCESTORS

As I've explained, it is our duty as the living to send the love and respect to our ancestors that they need in order to proceed happily through the afterworld.

When people die their memory will, with time, fade a little from the minds of their families, who must after all get on with life. This is to be expected. It is important though that they are not forgotten entirely.

I am not suggesting that we should be eternally heartbroken by the loss of loved ones, simply that we should remember them on certain days, such as the anniversaries of their deaths.

In Japan, the summer festival of Obon and the spring and autumn equinoxes are set aside for the remembrance of the dead. Other countries may have different customs, but there will always be a day that marks the anniversary of a loved one's death. No matter where you are or what your religion, you can have a kind thought for your loved ones on that day.

Remember your loved ones, even for a moment, and talk to them. Find a space somewhere on a shelf or a table to place a flower for them. Water is another offering all spirits are happy to receive. If your loved one was an avid reader, try leaving a few of his favorite books out as you think of him. If she was a woman who enjoyed dressing up and going out, place her foundation and lipstick somewhere in a similar way.

Every time you do this, you are creating a moment of sharing between yourself and the loved one who has passed away. No spirit will find your offerings unnecessary nor think them a nuisance. Every spirit loves to be cared for in this way.

When you place your hands together in prayer and think of people close to you who have left this world, you are in effect communicating with their spirits. Your actions will encourage them to help you in any way they can.

○○○○

Elaborate ceremony has no meaning when it comes to caring for the spirits. No matter what your religion, you can best look after them yourself. I myself belong to no religious group, and everything I have suggested in these pages has been passed on to me by my younger brother. He has never voiced any dissatisfaction with my actions regarding the spirits; on the contrary, after I have made an uncomplicated but significant offering such as the one that is described here, he always sends his thanks.

THE PRIESTS OF THE FRENCH REVOLUTION

An hour-and-a-half's drive out of Paris, in a lonely outer suburb where one would hardly expect to find such a historic building, stand the ruins of an old abbey. During the French Revolution, a large number of priests were sitting down to their morning meal in the refectory when the building was blown apart by bombs, just as they were saying grace. No one survived the attack.

The refectory was in the basement. It was already dark, and the moonlight was all we had to guide us. After walking down five or six crumbling steps we found a low-ceilinged room. I was traveling with a group of friends, and nervously we entered together. The basement itself was pitch black.

No one spoke, we were all too nervous. Trembling, we held onto each other, not one of us brave enough to venture farther into the room.

"Mrs. Gibo," someone finally whispered, "I think we should find out more about what's here." I agreed, adding that the tragic history of the abbey was a definite incentive to explore further.

We were interrupted by a sound. A piano could be heard.; someone was playing hymns.

I was the first to open my mouth. "Can you hear it, the piano?" I asked. The friend standing beside me nodded, then replied, her voice unsteady,

"Yes I can. What could the music be?"

No sooner had the words left her mouth that someone else

○○○○

said, "But there's nothing here: no houses even, so there can't be any pianos. So what is making this sound...?"

By now there was no doubt: we could all hear hymns being played nearby. Suddenly a voice spoke to us out of the darkness. For a split second I felt as if my heart had stopped beating.

"It was a terrible tragedy. Some of the priests were only in their teens, and their lives were snuffed out like candles, in an instant. We had done nothing to be killed, we died for no reason. Please, pray for us here. Understand how we feel. Help our souls to find rest."

The voice of a man in his sixties resounded in my head. I can speak no French. Yet I had been listening to a French priest.

At times like this I remember that no matter what nationality a spirit may be, communication between minds will overcome the language barrier and ensure that the message gets through.

We walked back up the stairs and out onto the moonlit lawn, and facing the church, prayed for some time for the souls of the priests. Once again I heard the voice, this time thanking us for our "kind prayer." Never had I experienced such profound communication with a spirit of a different religious belief.

WE OWE OUR EXISTENCE TO OUR ANCESTORS

Never forget, we owe our presence on this earth to our ancestors. The ancestors who help us in times of trouble are not the ones from many generations back. Most of those have already been reincarnated and are once more living on this earth. It is to our forbears of three or four generations ago that we should make the kind of offerings I have suggested.

It is important to remember when doing this that no matter how indifferent toward religion you yourself may be, if the spirit to whom you are speaking was a person of deep religious conviction, you must show respect for that. If, for example, the person concerned was a devout Christian, then it will be a great comfort to the spirit if you finish your communication with a sincere "Amen."

oooo

When the strength of the spirits is added to our own, we may experience the kind of miracle that leads us to believe that some supernatural power is assisting us. As human beings we are weak and often confused. But if we take care of our ancestors, they will come to us in our hour of need and inspire us with an idea which will lead the way out of our troubles.

There is no need to hesitate—start looking after your departed loved ones today.

THE OLD WEST APPEARED IN THE BACKGROUND

During my travels in the United States I met a woman by the name of Lucy. In her mid-thirties, she had a strong face matched by an equally strong personality. Lucy had no relatives apart from the older sister with whom she lived.

When she sat down, a scene began to appear behind her, a scene familiar to any fan of Westerns. A man, gaunt and tired, was walking along under the blazing sun, a large bag over his shoulder. From his appearance it was obvious that his life had been one of constant hard manual labor.

As he walked, a cloud of dust rose behind him. Through the dust I could make out a row of houses of the type commonly seen in Westerns, with steps leading up to spacious front porches.

As I started to describe the scene to Lucy, there was a sudden change. A dusty street once again appeared, but this time the houses were in ruins. There was still a man in the picture, and though of a stockier build than his predecessor, his face was very similar.

The scene was obviously set somewhere in the western United States, but where exactly was it, I wondered. And then a spirit voice began whispering slowly in my right ear, "Arizona, Arizona."

"Lucy," I asked, "do you have any connection with, or know anything about Arizona?"

"My mother apparently said that my grandfather was in

○○○○

Arizona," she replied. "But I was only a child when I was separated from her, so I can't be sure. I must admit though, the word
Arizona does have a familiar ring to it somehow."

Impatient as always at these times, I wanted to know exactly
where in Arizona this place was, and its name. I could now see
another row of buildings, this time of much more solid construc-
tion.

Closing my eyes for a while, I asked my brother, "Masao,
what's the name of this place with the sturdy buildings? I don't
suppose you'll be able to help me; after all, we are in the United
States here, but if you do know, could you tell me?" So saying, I
began rubbing my hands up and down my thighs, preparing to receive a message.

THIS WAS WHERE LUCY'S FOREBEARS HAD LIVED

Two or three minutes passed. Suddenly, the picture I had seen before reappeared. This time, however, I was able to spot the name
"Los Angeles" on a sign outside a bar.

"Ah, Los Angeles!" I exclaimed, before I lost the name. "Lucy,
do you have any memories of Los Angeles?"

"My sister told me that our family lived there a long time ago,
actually. Mrs. Gibo, both Arizona and Los Angeles are places my
ancestors have lived! That's amazing!" Her eyes shone with de-
light.

"Yes, Lucy, you're absolutely correct," I replied, relieved. "I'm
glad you were able to work that out so quickly."

When scenes appear behind a person like this, they are almost
certain to depict a place where the person's ancestors have lived or
where they are buried.

Why do the spirits cause such scenes to appear before me? It is
how they express their attachment to the place they once lived in.
I turned back to Lucy, and asked if she had ever visited her ancestors' graves.

"What? But my sister is the only living relative I know. She can

OOOO

remember my mother well and often talks about her....I must admit it makes me feel rather lonely to think that I don't know anything about my ancestors or what kind of life they led." She sat with her eyes downcast.

"Lucy," I continued, "life is not going very well for you at the moment, is it?"

"You're right there. Nothing goes well for me. Work most of all...I've always loved doing people's hair for them, so I got a hairdressing qualification. But I didn't get on well with the other employees at the first place I worked at, and was tricked by a guy there. I had to leave, and wandered from state to state for a while. I washed dishes, I worked as a maid...but never managed to get on with any of my bosses. The harder I try, the worse things get.

"It's a bit embarrassing to talk about really, but at one stage I even joined a weird black magic sect. Things began to go downhill even faster after that.

"A friend asked me if I wanted to go to San Francisco with her. She said she had a good job there, and that she'd get me one as well. That didn't work out either. I can stay with her until next month, but then I have to go, without a cent to my name.

"My sister and I are both Christians. Perhaps I'm being punished by God, what do you think? I can't imagine why else I'd be having bad luck all the time. I couldn't wait to meet you so I could ask."

My reading told me that Lucy came from a family that had never managed to own its own property. The man who had appeared in the Arizona scene was her great-grandfather, who I thought at first had been a slave: he owned no clothing, his skin was burnt to a coppery brown by the sun, and his thin body—that looked as if it could break in two any minute—was obviously suffering from malnutrition.

The man in the Los Angeles scene was his son: Lucy's grandfather. Like his father, I realized, he had never owned a home, and had lived out his days in poverty. What both of them wanted from Lucy was clear—a kind thought and a prayer.

○○○○

LUCY SENDS A MESSAGE TO HER ANCESTORS

"Lucy," I began again, "I want you to listen carefully and not misunderstand what I say here. Your ancestors worked very hard to try and build a better future for their children, but in the end they were unable to escape from poverty and were buried in Arizona and Los Angeles.

"This is your chance to make them happy. Put your hands together just as you usually do when you pray, and have a kind thought for them. In the mornings, try to imagine that there are two more people living in your apartment apart from yourself and your sister, and put out a piece of toast on a plate and perhaps small glasses of juice or cups of coffee. On a corner of the table will do. And don't forget to say good morning to both of them, out loud."

"Do I say 'Amen' then?"

"No, Lucy," I continued, "this is something completely separate from your religious beliefs. This has no connection with Christ or the Virgin Mary—think of it as a different kind of prayer entirely.

"I want you to think of the souls of your grandfather and great-grandfather as being by your side constantly. If you do as I've suggested then I believe your life will change for the better, because your grandfather and great-grandfather will become your guardian spirits.

"They'll be moved by the care you're taking to please them, and do their best to help you—when you think you've reached the limit of your own strength they'll be there to lend you a hand. Please, give my suggestions a try."

I must have spoken to her for an hour about the spirits: why there was nothing to fear from them, and how her own actions would determine whether they would protect her or not.

She thanked me for my advice.

"I've got it, Mrs. Gibo. When I feel like I can't cope I should ask my grandfather to help me: that's right, isn't it?" she asked,

○○○○

taking care to make sure she had fully understood me.

Six months later, I visited San Francisco again on business. I managed to meet one of Lucy's friends and asked how she was getting on.

"She's brightened up immeasurably," was the cheerful reply. "She 's doing everything you suggested, and she's really conscientious."

CARING FOR YOUR ANCESTORS EVERY DAY

The term "religious boom" has been in vogue in Japan for several years now, and stories abound of people frightened into spending vast amounts of money "consoling the spirits of their ancestors," —even those already reincarnated—having been persuaded that they will be inviting eternal bad luck if they neglect to do so. In the same way, countless women have been told that unless they pay to have prayers said for each fetus they have aborted, they and their entire family will die.

Whenever I hear of people being tricked in this way I see red. The spirits are not as malicious as some would have us believe. Our ancestors are happiest when receiving those thoughts and simple offerings we send them each day, and when I see people paying large amounts of money for the supposed consolation of spirits to the extent of having nothing left with which to enjoy life or, in the worst cases going into debt, I have to wonder why on earth they do it.

Money put aside for the souls of aborted children or for prayers for ancestors many generations back would be better spent, I believe, on preventing war. One way is to teach our children about the folly of man's desire to destroy others of his species. Our ancestors would be overjoyed if we did this.

Religion provides human beings with the strength to deal with the difficulties they encounter in their lives, and it is a noble thing to believe in any kind of god. If ever you are told, however, and start to believe that you must act in a certain way or your family

○○○○

will become ill or be visited by bad fortune, you should think carefully about your beliefs.

Show your children and grandchildren how to take care of their forebears. You will never regret it.

NEVER SAY HURTFUL THINGS TO A SPIRIT

There are several mistakes you should avoid making when you deal with the spirits. One of these is to verbally abuse the spirit of a person whom you never got along with, instead of saying a kind word to it. Spirits are paying for their past misdeeds already, in the spirit world, without their misery being compounded by the words of the living.

Crimes committed in this world are magnified tenfold in significance in the spirit world. Overwhelmed by a remorse they would not have thought imaginable while alive, the spirits of persons who have committed crimes are tormented, body and mind, by feelings which no matter how they try to suppress simply will not leave them in peace. This is "hell" as I described it in an earlier chapter, and there is no need for those who are left behind to twist the knife in the wounds of those who are already suffering for their misdeeds.

Offering food to the spirits which they were unable to eat while alive is another thing one should never do.

I once had an acquaintance who hated fish. I have yet to meet another person who loathed of it as he had done: even one piece on the table was enough to make him feel ill.

Thinking that he might grow to like it after his death, the man's family put some on the table for him one night when they were eating . They could not have been more mistaken.

That night the man's spirit appeared to his daughter in a dream, saying, "You know I can't stand the smell of that stuff: if you're going to put it there I'm afraid I won't be able to join you at mealtimes."

Years of working with spirits have shown me that the foods

○○○○

and interests which people enjoyed when they were alive, are the ones they continue to enjoy in the afterlife.

Another important aspect of making offerings to the spirits concerns the vessels that are used. Make sure that the cup into which you pour their tea or coffee is not cracked or otherwise damaged. Your offerings are their greatest pleasure, and no spirit will be happy to know that it is not even worth an undamaged cup.

AN EXPRESSION OF YOUR LOVE FOR THE SPIRITS

Jewelry is often offered to the spirit of a person who enjoyed wearing it on the anniversary of that person's death. Whatever you do, however, do not just casually take out the person's jewelry box and leave it somewhere without a great deal of thought. Instead, choose a piece or pieces which suited the person particularly well. The person's spirit will be greatly moved by the care you have taken.

One thing you should never offer a spirit is shoes. Even if they were the person's favorite pair, you have no way of knowing what they might have been in contact with outside, and thus they are an unsuitable offering.

The spirit of a person who died in summer will be grateful for a glass of water, while that of someone who died in winter will prefer something hot to drink: the odds are that if the person who died of an illness, he or she will have called for one or the other immediately before death.

Do not make the mistake, however, of offering medicines, or even the packet they have come from, to spirits of persons who died after a long illness. They will have no wish to be reminded of their lengthy struggle with death.

On the contrary, they will be thrilled to receive offerings of food which they loved to eat when they enjoyed good health, and anything they may have found pleasure in using such as a harmonica, a tennis racquet, or tapes of recorded music.

○○○○

Some people become anxious about making offerings, and think that they have to wash the dishes used for them separately, and use separate cloths to wipe them. There is no need for such measures—those dishes should be treated just the same as the ones used by the living. The important thing is to feel at ease about looking after your ancestors; all they want, after all, is for you to think of them as still being part of the family.

FOLLOW THE LAST WISHES OF YOUR LOVED ONES

The methods by which people want their bodies to be disposed of after death are many and varied. Some wish their ashes to be dropped from a plane into the sea, others want their bodies to be buried at sea, and there are even those who want their bodies to be fed to animals.

Anxious relatives come to me often with the question, "Is this really the correct way to do things?" to which I reply that there is no better way to dispose of a person's body than the way the person had wanted it to be done.

In many countries the law places certain restrictions on the methods by which bodies may be disposed of, but fulfilling the wishes of the deceased persons is still the best method, because then they will proceed into the spirit world satisfied that their burial was as they wanted it to be.

One of my friends was a woman who loved spending time alone. She found it troublesome and stressful to talk to her family, let alone her friends, and her greatest pleasure was to sit in a corner by herself with a book. As she put it,

"Nothing on earth could be better than reading a book while listening to the sound of leaves falling off a tree."

She died suddenly in her thirties; she had written in the diary that she wanted to be buried alone, away from other people. She could not bear the thought of her ashes being placed in a crowded cemetery.

Her family, however, ignored her wishes: they had a burial

○○○○

ground which had been in the family for generations and saw no reason not to place her remains there.

A year later, all four remaining members of the family had the same dream. In it the dead woman was covering her ears and saying that she could not bear the sound of people talking around her, and she pleaded to be placed somewhere on her own.

Still they ignored her plea, dismissing their identical dreams as a coincidence. Suddenly three of them began to complain of blinding headaches, and finally realized that they must shift the woman's remains. After buying a burial plot which was going cheaply due to its out-of-the-way location in the nearby mountains, they put her ashes there, and the headaches ceased immediately.

CHOOSE A BURIAL PLOT THAT COMPLIES WITH THE WISHES OF THE DEPARTED

It often happens that one partner in a marriage expresses the desire for a divorce, which is ignored by the other, or that a couple become tangled up in the law, resulting in a marriage that is a partnership in name only. It is generally assumed that a couple should be buried side by side, but in such cases it is probably preferable that they not be buried together.

The afterlife is long, and we should do what we can to make a spirit's journey through it as comfortable as possible. Realistically, this may well include burying people separately from partners with whom they did not get along.

While we are still fit and able, we should let our families know how we wish our bodies to be disposed of. Make a joke about it if you feel more at ease that way, but be sure your family knows what your wishes are.

There are those among us who would like to be in the midst of the bustle of everyday life, those who would prefer a quieter spot, those who love the mountains, others who love the sea, and yet others who would like to look over the place where they live. Part

○○○○

of making life after death as pleasant as possible is ensuring that people are buried in an environment close to that which they most loved while alive. A friend of mine who enjoys living in her apartment block told me she wanted her ashes to be placed in a crypt with those of others so she would not feel lonely. If that is really her wish, then every means should be used to carry it out.

Do not be afraid to say what you want people to do with your body after your death: your place of burial will play an important role in your life after death, so it is important not to choose just any crypt or make casual remarks about having your body dumped somewhere after your death.

Changing residences while you are alive is relatively simple, but any moving of your remains after death must be carried out entirely by other people, so make sure your wishes are clear while you are alive.

PETS MUST NOT BE BURIED WITH THEIR MASTERS

Animals and humans sense each other's moods. They comfort each other and love each other with such a depth of feeling that pets are often considered part of the family. What we must never forget, however, is that we as humans were born to inhabit a higher plane of existence than animals.

During our lives we learn many lessons and must do many things, not all of them pleasant. On the other hand, we are able to feel happiness in ways that no animal ever can.

Just as the worlds in which human beings and animals exist are different, so are the worlds they go to after death. The length of time that animals spend in the spirit world is much shorter than that of humans, in other words, they are reincarnated far more quickly than we are.

Our family always kept cats and dogs, and naturally each had a name. My brother tells me what has happened to them since they left this world.

"That little dog with the fluffy white coat you kept when you were young, it's leading another happy life now," he will say. Or, "That tabby cat by the name of Miko that you had, she's been re-born as a very clever animal, and her owners look after her well."

Along with these snippets of news about the pets I have loved over the years always comes a warning: animals should never be buried next to humans. They are on a different plane of existence from humans, my brother tells me, and no matter how much you loved them, they have an afterlife of their own to go to.

It was a long time before I myself accepted this, because the cat I had kept as a child always seemed more like a sister to me than a pet, and I never thought of her as an animal. It was the same even after she died.

Burying pets with their owners, however, is hard on the animals. Conscious of having to be careful of how they act around human beings, pets are easily tired. Moreover, the feelings that humans have toward the animals they loved change dramatically after death. When a person dies he or she realizes that there is a separate afterlife for pets, and that it is a great mistake it is to bury them with humans.

Animals should have their own burial grounds, which should be of a considerably lower standard than those of humans. If your pet dies, do everything you can to insure that it reaches the spirit world as quickly as possible. Different cultures have different customs regarding the burial of animals, and following them is the most certain way of assuring the animal's happiness.

The main thing to remember is that animals and humans are different and should be treated as such. I had a friend who kept a large dog. The dog was very clever, and was loyal to the family. It could even be sent on errands to the butcher or the fishmonger with only a note in its mouth. Needless to say the family treated it like a brother or sister.

When the dog died after a long and happy life, the family was heartbroken. It was as if one of them had passed away, and accordingly they buried it in the family plot.

○○○○

Nothing went well for them after that. Although they had always gotten along with each other quite well, the daughter, who was twenty-three, suddenly left home after a minor argument. Even more tragically, the twelve-year-old son was killed in an accident. The boutique that the couple owned had always been the envy of their neighbors, but suddenly they found themselves in the red. The family truly seemed to be plagued by misfortune.

I met with the couple, suspecting that their troubles sprang from the way they had buried the dog. At first they were reluctant to believe me, but as their adversities continued, they decided to try removing the dog's remains from the family plot and placing them in an animal cemetery. The results were immediate: the daughter who had left home returned, and laughter was heard once more in the house. Business began to pick up, not in a spectacular way, but it improved nonetheless, and the family could see in the future a return to the prosperity they had once known.

I love animals myself and so am prone to treating them like humans. It's been difficult at times, but I have tried to overcome this tendency and listen to the advice of my brother. Animals are indeed a lower form of life than humans, but this does not mean it is acceptable to mistreat them. Never forget that animals, no matter how small, have souls, and their feelings of gratitude toward kind owners will be carried over after death. A pet may even become his owner's guardian spirit, as in the case of the Landis's dog Daniel. Keep these facts in mind during your day-to-day encounters with animals.

DRIVEN TO OVEREATING

While on the subject of animals, I must tell you about a case I will never forget. The story concerns a woman by the name of Masai, who suffered from a serious eating disorder. The terms anorexia and bulimia are normally associated with teenage girls, but this woman, at the age of sixty-two, came to me with the following problem.

○○○○

"I eat six or seven times a day—all my savings have been spent on food, as well as the money from my husband's life insurance [he had died several years earlier]. What on earth should I do?"

I listened to her story in amazement. I'd never heard anything quite like this before, particularly from a woman of her age.

Masai had not always had this problem. On the contrary, until three years or so after her husband died she had if anything eaten less than most other people. A slice of toast for breakfast, a modest lunch and dinner.

"Then I started having these strange symptoms," she continued. "My hands and feet start to shake uncontrollably, and I feel incredibly hungry. A few minutes after eating, though, I want to be sick."

Masai had no children, but had lived a peaceful thirty years with her kind and hard-working husband and had nursed him through the illness which finally claimed his life. When he died, she told me, it simply felt as if the right time had come, and there was little shock to her system.

"I honestly can't think of any reason for me to become like this," she continued, obviously at the end of her tether. "I used to spend my days quite happily, making lace curtains and tablecloths as I'd always done, and now this all of a sudden...."

As she spoke, an interesting picture appeared behind her. As always, it looked as if it were on a television screen, apart from the faded colors. I began to describe what I saw.

"A girl of about ten is leading a horse. It's raining, and the rain is getting heavier. The road is no more than a footpath between rice paddies, and in the distance there is a forest, which is somewhat dark. It is wintertime, early in the evening.

"The road starts to wash away under the driving rain, and the girl, who looks poor, seems to have lost her way. The rain continues to get worse."

Masai was listening intently to every word, a look of disbelief on her face. I continued.

○○○○

"The girl, dressed in a plain kimono that looks like it has been washed many times and a short jacket, pulls on the reins with all her might but is unable to stop the horse from slipping into a rice paddy. She starts to cry, calling out for help. But no one hears, and she is powerless to do anything except watch the horse, its poor back bent under the heavy load, slipping slowly into the rice paddy.

"The picture finishes there—I have no idea what happened to the girl or her horse after that."

A HEARTRENDING STORY

My vision appeared to have triggered something in the woman's memory. As I finished, she burst into tears.

"I've tried so hard to forget that day, without success. It comes back to me sometimes, just as painful as all those years ago.

"I was the eldest of six children. My father died young, so it was up to my mother and me to carry on his work. He had worked as a wagon driver, loading goods onto a large wagon and hitching a horse to it. I was too small to load things on the wagon, so I generally ended up putting them straight on the horse's back.

"One evening I had finished work and was leading the horse home, the following day's deliveries on its back, when it started to rain. What you've just seen is exactly what happened that day. That horse, which had worked loyally for years, died, and there was nothing I could do."

That was as far as she got. Falling to the floor she continued to cry, her body heaving and shuddering with the enormity of her grief.

The year must have been about 1935, when people all over the world were living from hand to mouth. I could imagine how difficult it must have been for the woman who lay crying in front of me: left at the age of ten to support her brothers and sisters at a time when even families with two adult breadwinners were finding it hard to make ends meet.

At that time Masai was employed in Yokohama, where her

OOOO

father had worked for many years as what nowadays we would call a truck driver. Unlike now, however, work was done by horse, not truck, and the little girl was totally dependent on the young animal her father had left behind.

The animal was really little more than a foal, and was certainly not old enough to manage comfortably the loads it was called on to carry. At its young mistress's urging, however, it would stagger along, barely visible under the pile of baggage heaped on its back. No one seeing the young girl pulling the reins of the gallant little horse struggling under its huge load could fail to be moved to tears.

Who could really blame the loss of the horse on a child who was unable even to load the animal properly, let alone summon the strength to pull it out of the mud? Even I, who had listened to many sad stories, felt a lump in my throat.

THE HORSE WAS SEEKING ATTENTION

"Masai, you may find this hard to believe," I began, "but that horse is seeking some attention from you. Please, try putting out a bowl of water and perhaps some carrots, or other food the horse liked, on your kitchen table, and saying a prayer of thanks to it. It was obviously a clever animal, so I think it will understand your feelings. You'll also find that your eating problems will be eased by this."

She eagerly promised to do as I suggested. A week later, she came to see me again and related excitedly how her appetite had returned to normal that day. I met her once more, several years later.

"My problem just went away after that," she told me with a smile. "And I still make offerings to the horse sometimes."

Some of you will no doubt find it hard to believe there is such a thing as consoling the spirits of animals as we do those of humans, but countless examples prove otherwise.

That hard-working little horse must be due by now to join us

○○○○

on earth again. With any luck it will enjoy a happier life this time around.

ᴵᴵᴵᴵ|| 11 ||ᴵᴵᴵ
YOUR
GUARDIAN SPIRIT

THINGS TO DO IF YOU WANT YOUR GUARDIAN SPIRIT TO PROTECT YOU

As I have shown in the preceding chapters, enjoying the protection of a guardian spirit can make a great difference in our lives. For our guardian spirit to be willing to help us when we need it, we ourselves must possess the kind of soul it approves of. What does this mean specifically?

The first "rule," if you like, in gaining the approval and assistance of your guardian spirit, is to avoid all feelings of despair. Worrying about things that have not yet happened, and even worse that may never happen, is one of the things that guardian spirits dislike the most. Be cheerful, be forward-thinking, be sure of your own feelings. Only then will your guardian spirit come to your side.

FINDING YOUR GUARDIAN SPIRIT

I'm sure everyone would like to know just who their guardian spirit is. Finding out is not particularly difficult.

When you have a spare moment, close your eyes and think of individuals close to you who have passed away. The image of your guardian spirit as it flashes in your mind is one you will never forget. You will recall the person concerned vividly, even down to his or her mannerisms. If your mind is suddenly flooded with memories of a particular person in this way, it is no coincidence. It is because the person is close to you. Without a doubt, you will have discovered the identity of your guardian spirit.

"PLEASE BE MY GUARDIAN SPIRIT"

Perhaps you would like someone in particular to become your guardian spirit—a person of ability, someone who had been an intelligent and respected member of the community. It can be done.

The person will probably have been a relation or friend, or maybe a teacher. Speak to the person, think of him or her and ask

○○○○

the person to be your guardian spirit. Spirits are benevolent beings: if you really wish them to help you, they will listen to your request.

It is even possible, though rare, for a person whom you have never actually met to become your guardian spirit, if your desire for that person's protection is strong enough.

One thing to remember: you cannot always expect to be on the receiving end of the spirits' generosity. You must give as well— pray that their journey through the afterworld will pass smoothly, and when you take time out for a cup of tea or coffee, remember to put some aside for them. Have a kind thought for the person whom you wish to be your guardian spirit when you do this, and you will be creating the kind of environment in which the spirit feels comfortable enough to draw close to you.

When your guardian spirit chooses to stay with you at all times, you will become aware of a change in your life not unlike coming out of a bitterly cold winter into a spring of warm sun and abundant flowers.

Your guardian spirit will help you through major life crises, and you will find potential disasters being reduced to minor problems. If, for example, you are involved in an accident which by rights should have left you with serious injuries, you may escape with only a few scratches. I know of many such cases.

EXPRESS YOUR THANKS OUT LOUD

Receiving messages from your guardian spirit will be easiest if you think of that spirit often and ask for its help. It will respond to your sincerity. Do not let any other thoughts enter your head while you think of your guardian spirit. If human beings concentrate their thoughts hard enough, they have the potential to overcome any barrier, physical or otherwise. And it is most important that you do not forget to express your thanks out loud when you have received assistance from your guardian spirit.

If you do that, a time will come when you have "premonitions" concerning events about to take place. You may feel uneasy about going somewhere or doing something, or your guardian spirit may appear in a dream to warn you of impending disaster.

The relationship between ourselves and our guardian spirits is essentially one of give and take. We cannot expect their help if we neglect our duty as the living to take care of them.

The spirits are also more likely to assist people who are optimistic and forward-thinking, as opposed to those who have become consumed by hate, resentment, and jealousy. If you display the latter traits, you are likely to find your guardian spirit abandoning you.

No matter what happens, be grateful that you are alive, and make your best effort in all your endeavors. When the power of your guardian spirit is added to this, nothing will be able to keep you down for long.